All the King's Horses

Essays on the Impact of Looting
and the Illicit Antiquities Trade
on Our Knowledge of the Past

Edited by Paula K. Lazrus and Alex W. Barker

SOCIETY FOR AMERICAN ARCHAEOLOGY
The SAA Press

The Society for American Archaeology, Washington, D.C. 20005
Copyright © 2012 by the Society for American Archaeology
All rights reserved. Published 2012
Printed in the United States of America

Printed on acid-free paper

Library of Congress Cataloging-in-Publication Data

All the king's horses : essays on the impact of looting and the illicit
antiquities trade on our knowledge of the past / edited by Paula Kay Lazrus
and Alex W. Barker. -- Rev. ed.
   p. cm.
Includes bibliographical references and index.
ISBN 978-0-932839-44-2 (alk. paper)
1. Antiquities--Collection and preservation--Moral and ethical aspects. 2.
Historic sites--Conservation and restoration--Moral and ethical aspects. 3.
Cultural property--Protection--Moral and ethical aspects. 4. Archaeological
thefts. 5. Pillage. 6. Archaeology--Moral and ethical aspects. 7.
Archaeology--Political aspects. 8. Archaeology--Law and legislation. I.
Lazrus, Paula Kay. II. Barker, Alex W.
   CC135.A458 2012
   930.1--dc23
                    2012005764

Contents

1 *All the King's Horses*: An Introduction   1
   Alex W. Barker and Paula Kay Lazrus

2 The Economics of the Looted Archaeological Site   9
   of Bâb edh-Dhrâ': A View from Google Earth
   Neil Brodie and Daniel A. Contreras

3 The Material and Intellectual Consequences   25
   of Acquiring the Sarpedon Krater
   David Gill

4 Moot Loot Speaks: Classical Archaeology   43
   and the Displaced Object
   Stephen L. Dyson

5 Unprovenienced Artifacts and the Invention of Minoan   55
   and Mycenaean Religion
   Senta C. German

6 Early Looting and Destruction of Australian   71
   Shipwreck Sites: Legislation, Education, and an
   Amnesty for Long-Term Preservation
   Jennifer Rodrigues

7 The Trade in Fresh Supplies of Ancient Coins:
   Scale, Organization, and Politics   91
   Nathan T. Elkins

8	The Social and Political Consequences of Devotion to Biblical Artifacts *Neil Brodie and Morag M. Kersel*	109
9	What *All the King's Horses* Has to Say to American Archaeologists *Ann M. Early*	127

References Cited	133
About the Contributors	157
Index	159

1

All the King's Horses: *An Introduction*

ALEX W. BARKER *and* PAULA KAY LAZRUS

A wise old egg once said that words mean exactly what we choose for them to mean, nothing more and nothing less.[1] It is therefore worthwhile taking a few moments at the outset to define what this volume is all about.

All the King's Horses was originally conceived as a reflection on the effects of looting and distortion of the archaeological record, on the irretrievable loss of the evidence of our common, shared human past. While at first glance that seems a simple statement of which even Humpty-Dumpty could be proud, there are some uncomfortable truths lurking beneath the surface of those words.

For all our rhetoric about studying the past, that's not really what archaeologists do, except in a vague and imprecise manner of speaking. The past is, for good or ill, beyond our reach, a profoundly different and distant place that we can explore only through memory of lived experience, imagination, or a few relatively rare bits of evidence—artifacts or ecofacts, soil stains or settlement patterns, and surviving texts, among others. The past is passed, already gone. What survives, and what this book is ultimately concerned with, are those bits of the past that have somehow escaped the ravages of time, processes of decay, and the constant tug of entropy to survive into the present. We don't—can't—study the past directly. Instead, we study the present, and those bits of the past that survive into the present, to make inferences about that past. Whether or not those inferences are valid depends in large part on how carefully we've examined and interrogated those bits of the past. The fact that we cannot study the past directly does not mean that the past is in any sense unknowable, however, but instead, that our ability to understand the past is intrinsically dependent on and constrained by the evidence that survives. This is what makes those bits so precious—they represent our only tangible link to the past and our only means of creating and validly assessing our understandings of that past.

But whose past? Although some archaeologists might accept the notion of a common, shared human past, others would not. And some other communities of interest would reject the notion entirely, asserting the priority of both their claims to the past and the primacy of their interpretations of that past. These debates are played out at multiple levels, ranging from well-publicized struggles for contested objects to subtle and nuanced discussions within the discipline regarding the appropriateness of terms like *cultural resources* (which suggests exploitation and use) vs. *cultural heritage* (which suggests shared value and interest). Most of the essays in this volume examine, to greater or lesser degrees, competing claims to the past and its surviving fragments by groups who feel they enjoy a privileged claim, a priority that trumps the concerns, needs, or interests of others. Collectors, directors of "cosmopolitan" art museums, salvors, or treasure seekers, subsistence diggers, national governments, and descendant groups may all feel they have a vested interest in the past and a right to control its tangible (or intangible) remains. For some those interests are economic, for others aesthetic, experiential, cultural, or spiritual. It is worth noting, in that regard, that two elements set archaeological interests in the past apart from those of other groups.

First, archaeologists generally seek nonexclusive access. Many groups seek to control the past by restricting access to its tangible remains, claiming privileged rights to the past through descent, private ownership, religious affiliation, or patrimonial rule. Such privileged access brings with it control over how the fragments of the past are used, studied, or presented.[2] Such claims may further constrict the surviving evidence, limiting both who can study the remains and what kinds of conclusions they can draw from them. Archaeologists do not provide an exhaustive view of the past—as a discipline we don't have all the questions, much less all of the answers—and as a result archaeologists do not seek an exclusive right to interpret the past.

Second, and in a related vein, archaeological claims to the past seek the preservation of the maximum information possible about objects and their contexts; emphasizing the importance of archaeological context does not generally strip from objects other kinds of contextual information. Archaeological claims do not restrict or limit other uses, except to the degree that those other uses depend on exclusivity (such as certain patrimonial or property-based claims). They represent a bigger tent, allowing any nonexclusive use of objects, and preserving the maximum possible information about these bits of the past allows their use by a range of individuals, groups, or communities.

In some cases those bits are objects of remarkable beauty and are prized as works of art. Some would argue that these works carry within them all the context they need, and that archaeological protestations regarding in-situ context are superfluous or special pleading. They would argue that connoisseurship is enough, that exhaustive knowledge and a critical eye allows one to fill in the evidentiary gaps, creating a context for pieces whose archaeological context has been lost.

Yet, it seems clear that what is constructed through such means is not a valid context for the object except in the most trivial sense, but instead, simply reifies current assumptions and viewpoints. The context created is merely what we would expect that object's context to be if our current understanding was already correct and adequate.[3] Less scholarship than self-congratulation, this kind of shallow connoisseurship privileges existing conceptions over whatever valid knowledge an object might have helped reveal. And bits that happen to fall in a broader, less aesthetically attractive category—despite their profound importance for understanding the past—are too often lost as collateral damage.

None of this should be taken as a condemnation of true connoisseurship, of course. A trained and critical eye can enrich our understanding of the past, helping all of us see more clearly. But informed connoisseurship is premised on knowledge of context rather than on its rejection, adding to our knowledge of the past rather than preempting it. The biographies of these bits of the past are rich and nuanced, comprising both archaeological contexts *in* antiquity and their circulation after discovery *as* antiquities. Adequate biographies and the scholarship and connoisseurship giving rise to these biographies must include both. Preserving archaeological context makes an object no less beautiful, and no less amenable to aesthetic criticism and enjoyment.

By contrast, approaches that reject the necessity of archaeological context, that accept this collateral damage as the price of economically recovering choice works of art, or that see objects as inherently carrying their biographies with them create de facto exclusivity, restricting the use of objects to those groups or individuals who share that narrower vision of what kinds of inferences can or should be drawn from the tangible bits of the past that survive. Such approaches are narrower both in rejecting the range of inferences we can make about objects from their context and associations, from all the less spectacular bits of evidence yielded by archaeological deposits, but also in positing the context and significance of objects based on existing understandings (rather than using archaeological context to observe the actual provenience and observed significance of objects, which may be different than what is currently assumed); they rob from the past its ability to surprise us and to confound our expectations.

There is, however, one area in which archaeologists actively restrict the use of the past. Most archaeological organizations, including the Society for American Archaeology, restrict first publication of looted objects or objects bereft of context. One reason is that publication of looted objects may have the unintended effect of increasing the value or perceived authenticity of such objects and, hence, the scale of looting and site destruction. Certainly these are important and valid concerns, but they represent only part of the reason that objects with unknown provenience are shunned.

The other reason is that reconstructed contexts, those fictionalized biographies for objects that are based on our own assumptions and presumptions, are not only limited and narrow in the ways noted above, but also may create flawed foundations on which to build subsequent generations of scholarship. If our attributions or identifications prove incorrect—either in the immediate sense of admitting fakes into the corpus or in the more common but complicated sense of having misplaced an object because it really did indicate something new and unexpected—it becomes very difficult to recant, retract, or otherwise redeem the error. Worse still, it is often impossible to determine that the error took place at all, so that the validity of subsequent inferences cannot be adequately assessed.

But the discipline pays a high price for this surety. Important objects with limited or no provenience may be unreported as a result, a concern felt especially keenly by epigraphers and iconographers who fear that the loss of information from documents unreported or works unstudied because they are from looted contexts outweighs the dangers of misattributions. One of the key challenges facing the discipline in the decades to come is how to balance concerns about the use of looted objects on the one hand and the loss of knowledge from such objects left unpublished on the other. This is an admittedly difficult topic for archaeologists, however, as some (but not all) arguments for recognizing the value of information recoverable from undocumented antiquities are offered by those with a vested interest in supporting or benefiting from the continued trade in looted objects. And many archaeologists with long experience in the debate over undocumented antiquities see no practical way to allow publication of some undocumented antiquities but not others.

The original impetus for this volume was a session organized in 2008 at the Society for American Archaeology meeting in Vancouver, Canada. "All the King's Horses: Looted or Unprovenienced Artifacts and the Valid Construction of the Past" was organized by the Ethics Committee of the Society for American Archaeology to explore the impact of vandalism of archaeological sites and the traffic in antiquities not only on the sites themselves and the loss of interpretive context of the materials, but also on the corpus of archaeological knowledge as a whole. If many/most objects from a particular "culture" are unprovenienced, how does this affect our interpretations and understanding not only of the materials themselves but of the entire culture? How do we differentiate authentic from fake in the absence of demonstrable archaeological context? With these questions in mind, the Ethics Committee sponsored the forum, which was coorganized by Alex W. Barker and Paula Kay Lazrus. Some of the essays herein are developed from presentations at the forum, whereas others were solicited specifically for this volume.

The volume begins with a study examining the economics of looting. Neil Brodie and Daniel Contreras calculate the economic impact of looting at a single site, Bâb edh-Dhrâ' in Jordan, using freely available imagery through Google Earth. Their contribution provides a method for quantifying, using widely available technologies, both the extent of site destruction and the economic impact of looting activities at sites.

Classical archaeology's struggle to interpret and contextualize objects whose original context has been lost is examined in detail by Stephen Dyson. As a discipline, classical archaeology has faced the problem of objects without meaningful context since its inception, and much of its history can be understood as a series of attempts to create valid contexts to stand in for archaeological contexts now lost. David Gill next takes up the epic of the Sarpedon (aka Euphronios) krater, returned to Italy in

2008 by the Metropolitan Museum of Art. In many ways, the Sarpedon krater became the poster child for restitution efforts on the one hand and defenses by major institutions for accepting looted or undocumented antiquities on the other. Gill's essay distills broader arguments regarding undocumented antiquities down to essences embodied in the struggle for a single object and reveals the complex interests and agendas of leading figures in the debate.

In the following chapter Senta German explores the role of undocumented antiquities in the development of ideas of religion and belief in the Minoan and Mycenaean worlds. Misattributed objects or outright fakes played an important role in early conceptions of Minoan religion and social organization, illustrating clearly the ways in which unprovenienced artifacts can be fit into existing constructs that suit the taste of the times better than the past they seek to document. And as she also demonstrates, these misattributions and the intellectual traditions based on them can continue long after the initial errors are corrected.

Recognizing both the continuing threat to in situ archaeological resources and the potential information to be gained from materials looted from maritime sites, Australia offered an amnesty program in 1993–1994 for divers who had removed archaeological material from known wrecks. During this amnesty period individuals could declare objects taken from wrecks without fear of punishment or sanction. Jennifer Rodrigues examines both this amnesty program and the continuing complexities attendant on privately owned and partially regulated archaeological collections—an important and timely discussion as some Australian officials have begun to discuss another amnesty.

Nathan Elkins's contribution examines the trade in ancient coins, a category of antiquities that is traded relatively freely and openly and that boasts both a broad socioeconomic spectrum of collectors and a powerful lobby supporting its dealers. The status of coins as antiquities has become a volatile topic in recent years, following the addition of coins to the list of restricted antiquities under the renewal of the Cypriot bilateral agreement—the first time coins had been so listed.[4] Elkins both highlights some of the tactics used by the coin dealer lobby and makes a case for a more direct approach to the collectors themselves.

In the penultimate essay Neil Brodie and Morag Kersel explore the additional pressures placed on museums when the poorly provenienced object isn't simply a work of aesthetic beauty but purports to be a new-found artifact confirming religious beliefs. Their review of the case of the James Ossuary documents the struggles faced by the Royal Ontario Museum in deciding whether to display an ossuary whose provenience was unknown but whose blockbuster potential was clear. Their essay also highlights the power of the past to excite our imaginations and the ways in which this power can be used or abused.

Finally, Ann Early provides a brief Americanist perspective on the themes and problems raised in this volume.

Certainly, many of the issues and challenges considered here resonate as clearly with American archaeology as with archaeology as practiced overseas. At the same time, however, by focusing on these issues and challenges as they are perceived elsewhere, this volume may have special value for New World archaeologists. While similar, these issues and challenges are inflected differently in different areas, informed by different histories, and uniquely inscribed by how the past and its evidence is constructed, construed, articulated, and owned in different legal, social, and political contexts. Sovereignty, for example, has quite different connotations in the context of modern nation-states asserting rights to antiquities of any kind and relating to any group found within their borders, rather than in the context of sovereign tribes existing within a nation-state asserting rights to ancestral material through its internal legal frameworks. Similarly, cultural property has very different connotations for coin dealers asserting individual property rights and native communities asserting communal patrimonial rights—the same terms of art used with very different meanings, which continue to exist in parallel and competing ways within current U.S. law. These differing perspectives may help illuminate many of the knotty problems facing New World archaeology, offering both fresh viewpoints and the benefits of others' experience.

Certain themes raised in these chapters transcend borders. Methods for quantifying the scale of site looting and estimating its economic impact are of broad applicability and may be particularly useful to American archaeologists struggling with legal frameworks using the value of looted objects or cost of looting activities in assessing penalties. Ongoing debates regarding how to salvage information from collections pot-hunted or otherwise lacking provenience and provenance may find Australia's experience in collecting data through amnesty programs useful and relevant, and the social and financial pressures on museums to display compelling or popular objects regardless of how they were acquired are felt globally.

Most important, however, these essays help us think of archaeological remains in broader terms, not only as those rare and precious bits of the past that allow us to understand ancient communities and societies, but also as objects that, by perduring into the present, are affected by and partly constitutive of modern political, economic, and social contexts as well. Understanding the significance of these more modern aspects of an ancient object's biography remains a largely unexplored but compelling area for archaeological study.

Readers of *All the King's Horses* should be aware that it does not offer prescriptive solutions to problems. Yet, while there are few easy answers, the questions remain compelling and the need to address them is growing. The surviving fragments of the past are a finite resource, increasingly contested and increasingly at risk. Unless we find better and more effective ways of protecting the surviving fragments of antiquity, our ability to reconstruct the past may be lost forever, beyond the ability of either archaeologists or all the king's horses to recover.

Notes

1. Humpty Dumpty, in chapter 6 of Lewis Carroll's *Through the Looking Glass and What Alice Found There*.

2. Aptly captured by Carroll: "'The question is,' said Humpty Dumpty, 'which is to be master—that's all.'"

3. Our understanding of the past is neither, and that's why we grub about for those rare bits of the past, beautiful and otherwise, in the first place.

4. These agreements are the mechanism under existing U.S. law of implementing the 1970 UNESCO Convention on the Means of Prohibiting and Preventing the Illicit Import, Export and Transfer of Ownership of Cultural Property.

2

The Economics of the Looted Archaeological Site of Bâb edh-Dhrâ': A View from Google Earth

NEIL BRODIE *and* DANIEL A. CONTRERAS

Archaeological concern about the antiquities trade and associated looting of archaeological sites has generally focused on what have been termed its "material and intellectual consequences" (Gill and Chippindale 1993). In other words, on the destruction of archaeological materials and contexts caused by unsystematic and unrecorded removal, and on the misinterpretations and misunderstandings that are introduced into historical enquiry when decontextualized artifacts are received and studied as valuable and collectable art objects. More recently, however, the broader social and political consequences of the antiquities trade have also begun to attract attention, including its criminal involvement, the disrespect of sovereign rights, the corrosive effects of cultural loss on social memory and identity, the socioeconomic elitism of the collectors, and the socioeconomic deprivation of those who do the looting. This latter context is the one that concerns us here, and we present the results of a preliminary evaluation of the potential of Google Earth for producing quantitative data that might be used to investigate the comparative economics of the antiquities trade.

Subsistence Digging

The growing strand of concern about the poor socioeconomic circumstances of the people who do the actual looting can be traced back at least to Dwight Heath's (1973) sympathetic study of illicit excavation and trade in Costa Rica (see also Lange 1976). Then, in 1993, David P. Staley, disturbed by the use of pejorative terms such as *looting* to describe the actions of illicit excavators, coined the less judgmental "subsistence digging" to use instead. He defined a "subsistence digger" as "a person who uses the proceeds from artifact sales to support his or her traditional subsistence lifestyle" (Staley 1993:348). The use of the term *subsistence digging* is intended to avoid further stigmatizing people or communities already suffering from economic deprivation or from political discrimination or oppression, and to help recognize their right to economic self-determination (Hollowell 2006a, 2006b:72–73; Hollowell-Zimmer 2003; Matsuda 1998, 2005). Yet, while there is some measure of agreement within the archaeological community that the term *subsistence digging* is a useful one, there is uncertainty and disagreement about the limits of its applicability. Julie Hollowell (2006b:77), for example, rightly asks whether "subsistence" in the early twenty-first century should include such things as college education and the purchase of computers, although many would still baulk at any attempt to characterize the lifestyle of fast cars and women enjoyed by some Tuscan *tombaroli* (described by van Velzen 1996) as a subsistence one.

The identification of subsistence digging as an issue of economic justice has raised a number of questions about the economic value of archaeological heritage—about how economic value is constituted, how it is realized, and how it is distributed. Laws and ethical codes aimed at suppressing the illicit excavation and trade of archaeological heritage, and more generally at regulating ownership and access, typically avoid any productive engagement with economic value.[1] Although the intention of much heritage legislation is protective, its action is prophylactic, installing a legal barrier between the public and a cultural and economic resource. Yet, although such legislation attempts to place archaeological heritage outside the economic domain, the persistence of archaeological looting and the continuing trade in antiquities shows that it has not succeeded. Instead, economic value has become a covert value, shaping perceptions and offering opportunities for exploitation, while at the same time remaining outside the scope of any constructive discussion and normative or legislative intervention. It can even be argued that regulatory laws are failing in their purpose precisely because they omit to make any provision for the equitable distribution of economic value (Brodie 2010).

This denial of economic value by archaeological heritage law and ethics (and by art historical and archaeological scholarship more gener-

Table 1. *Initial Price of Artifact Paid to Finder and Price Paid for First Time on International Market.*

Artifact	Initial price	Final price	Time lapse (years)	References
Achyris (Steinhardt) phiale (1980, Italy)	$20,000	$1.2 million	11	Slayman 1998
Morgantina acroliths (1979, Italy)	$1100	$1 million	1	Robinson 1998
Statue of Marsyas (1988, Turkey)	$7400	$540,000	<6	Rose and Acar 1995
Euphronios krater (1971, Italy)	$8800	$1 million	1	Slayman 1998
Yongtai head (1996, China)	$840	$125,000	1	Maggio 1998
Amenhotep head (1991, Egypt)	$6000	$1.4 million	<3	Watson 2002, 26; Tokeley 2006, 202
Asteas krater (1970s, Italy)	A pig (!)	$275,000	<10	Slayman 2006
Nataraja (1982, India)	£12	£250,000	6	O'Keefe 1997, 19 n. 35
Morgantina silver (Italy)	$27,000	$3 million		Watson and Todeschini 2007, 106.

[handwritten margin note: "None are 'typical'."]

ally) also means that very little is known about it. Most policy suggestions in this area that consider economics are concerned to evaluate the applicability of simple or more sophisticated market models, which in themselves offer only a subset of possible economic solutions, and which are in any case vitiated by the general paucity and unreliability of empirical data that might be used to test them. The reasons for this data shortage are not hard to find. The funding and kudos attached to short-term, solution-oriented research is not forthcoming for more fundamental, difficult and long-term research into the nature of the problem for which solutions are sought. In such an under-researched environment, however, even well-meaning solutions have the potential to cause more harm than good. Cautionary admonitions about houses built on sand come to mind.

As an example, it is instructive to consider the discussion that has developed concerning the remuneration of subsistence diggers. The return on their labor appears poor when viewed in the context of the

```
Morgantina silver     0.9%
Nataraja              0.005%
Amenhotep head        0.4%
Yongtai head          0.7%
Euphronios krater     0.9%
Marsyas statue        1.4%
Morgantina acroliths  0.11%
Achyris phiale        1.7%
```

Figure 1. Percentage of price paid for an artifact on the international market received by finder (based on data in Table 1). *misleading.*

global antiquities market, but might be appreciable in local terms. There are few data available that describe the increasing prices of artifacts as they pass up the trading chain, but those that are available show that typically the diggers receive something like 1 percent of the international market value of a piece (Table 1; Figure 1). Although this statistic of 1 percent is derived from price data for "big ticket" items, similarly low percentages for more mundane objects have been suggested from Costa Rica (Heath 1973:261; Lange 1976:306), Turkey (Acar and Kaylan 1988), China (Boylan 1995:103), and Israel (Kersel 2006:164–166).

Against this evidence of low remuneration, Jerome C. Rose and Dolores L. Burke's (2004) systematic work in north Jordan suggested that diggers there were receiving a higher percentage of international market price. For example, on the ground, they were receiving $7 each for Roman oil lamps (Rose and Burke 2004:4) at a time when, in London, similar lamps were being sold for about $45 each (Brodie, personal observation). Thus, the diggers were receiving about 15 percent of the international market price. Hollowell has reported that St. Lawrence Island diggers, who corporately own the archaeological resource, and whose artifacts enter the market legally, can receive anything up to 70 percent of the international market price (Hollowell 2006a:121). This higher percentage return in a legal market suggests that the risks and expenses involved in transporting and "laundering" illegally acquired artifacts across international borders cause the large markups in price that occur between artifacts coming out of the ground and their final sale on the

right.

international market. What that means to the diggers in real terms, however, is not clear. It is possible that prices on the ground are not coupled to final prices on the international market, which are more likely to reflect the variable effects of transaction costs and demand. For example, in Belize, it is believed that the intensity of subsistence digging is linked to agricultural success or failure, not to prices on the international market (Matsuda 1998:94). But, although subsistence diggers or looters may be cheated out of the full value of their labor, it remains the case that because digging is usually illegal, and so not subject to taxation or profiteering employment practices, they might feel cheated less than in other—legitimate—employment.

Another line of discussion about the remuneration of subsistence digging concerns aggregate monetary incomes and economic outcomes. Archaeological heritage is a limited resource, and in the long term, digging is unsustainable as a subsistence option. Nonetheless, it might still be justified in socioeconomic terms if the income generated is used to establish a more permanent and improved source of income. So, for a hypothetical example, a digger might use money derived from the sale of artifacts to pay for a child to obtain a law degree. Whether such "wise investment strategies" actually exist, however, is another matter—there are no documented examples. Another relevant consideration is that money obtained through digging is ultimately derived from abroad, so in sufficient quantities it might constitute what in 2008 would have been called an "economic stimulus" for a local economy, with diffuse though positive effects. Dwight B. Heath, for example, in the early 1970s, reckoned that 1 percent of the economically active population of Costa Rica was directly involved in the antiquities trade, and that the trade generated about $500,000 per year for the Costa Rican economy (about 70 percent derived from abroad), which was further spread around through "wages, royalties, commissions, flim-flams, graft, and other kinds of exchanges" (Heath 1973:260). Hollowell estimated that every year dealers spend an estimated $1.5 million on St. Lawrence Island, which works out to be about $1,000 per inhabitant (Hollowell 2006a:105).

Again, Rose and Burke's (2004) work in north Jordan is an important reference point. They conducted an informal pedestrian survey of six Roman-Byzantine cemeteries in the Irbid-Ramtha area, counting 570 robbed tombs in total. They used this figure in conjunction with information about tomb contents derived from the literature and price information obtained from the diggers to conclude that even as a minimum estimate the contents of the robbed tombs would have generated on the ground something like $14,000 to $25,000 for each cemetery. Multiplying those figures by the 745 known Roman-Byzantine cemeteries in the area, Rose and Burke concluded that the sale of material from all cemeteries would make a total of between $10 to $18 million for the regional economy, ultimately earned from abroad.

Studies such as those conducted by Hollowell and Rose and Burke are important because they place looting/subsistence digging in a quantifiable economic context. It is only through such studies that progress will be made toward introducing sustainable and equitable strategies of economic exploitation of archaeological heritage as realistic alternatives to undocumented digging. With this pressing need for quantitative data in mind, we have investigated how estimates of site damage obtained from satellite imagery available on Google Earth can be combined with information derived from other sources to produce some (primitive) financial indicators.

The Contribution of Google Earth

In principle, looted archaeological sites and the amount of looting damage visible on individual sites can be identified and assessed remotely through the use of high-resolution aerial and/or satellite imagery. Up until the middle 2000s, however, the cost of obtaining up-to-date images of sufficiently high resolution was generally prohibitive. This situation improved in 2005 when the launch of Google Earth provided a platform, making low-cost, good-quality satellite imagery publicly available.

The imagery used on Google Earth derives from a number of sources and is variable in terms of date and resolution. Much imagery, particularly of remote areas, has a resolution of less than 30 m/pixel, although this is improving, and for many areas of the Earth's surface, image resolution is now better than 1 m/pixel (see Parcak 2009:43–51), which is suitable for identifying areas of ground disturbed by looting, although not usually for delineating individual pits. Most imagery is between one to three years old but is regularly updated, and since the release of Google Earth 5 in 2008, older images have been archived and made accessible so that in the future overviews of change over time will become increasingly viable.

We have recently completed a preliminary evaluation of Google Earth imagery for studying archaeological site looting in Jordan (Contreras and Brodie 2010). We chose Jordan for our preliminary study because archaeological looting there is well documented (Bisheh 2001; McCreery 1996; Politis 2002; Rose and Burke 2004), and geospatial data about archaeological site locations was publicly available in the form of the JADIS database. Furthermore, there was the important technical consideration that Google Earth incorporates, for much of Jordan, sub-meter/pixel visual spectrum imagery from the Quickbird satellite owned by the Digital-Globe corporation. It was not possible in the time available to subject all imaged terrain to visual inspection, and so two sampling strategies were implemented (see Contreras and Brodie 2010 for details). This enabled the identification of 25 sites that we considered to show evidence of looting (visible as pitting, which presented on the images as highly contrasting, intermingled dark and light pixels, distinct from the low-contrast background pixels). Subsequent ground-truthing established that 13 out of 16 sites visited showed evidence of recent digging, thus confirming the reliability of the method.

Image resolution for looted sites was generally not adequate to allow the identification of individual pits, and so counts of pit number and direct estimates of pit density were not possible. To quantify damage, then, we chose instead to measure total pitted area. Visibly disturbed areas identified as pitted were isolated with boundary polygons in ArcGIS, which in several cases entailed drawing multiple polygons for a single site. The resulting shapefile was then used to calculate the total pitted area. Of the 22 sites that after ground-truthing we believed to show evidence of looting, six were Early Bronze Age (EBA) in date, and EBA sites accounted for 68 percent of the total looted area of 515,351 m^2 (51.5 ha or ~.5 km^2). Furthermore, three of the four largest looted sites were the EBA cemetery sites of Bâb edh-Dhrâ', Fayfa', and an-Naq' in the area of Ghor es-Safi, southeast of the Dead Sea (Figure 2).

Bâb edh-Dhrâ'

The best known and most systematically excavated and published of the three EBA cemeteries is Bâb edh-Dhrâ'. Bâb edh-Dhrâ' has been known to archaeologists since at least 1924 when it was reported that several tombs there had been looted (Albright 1924:59). It was first excavated in

16 *All the King's Horses*

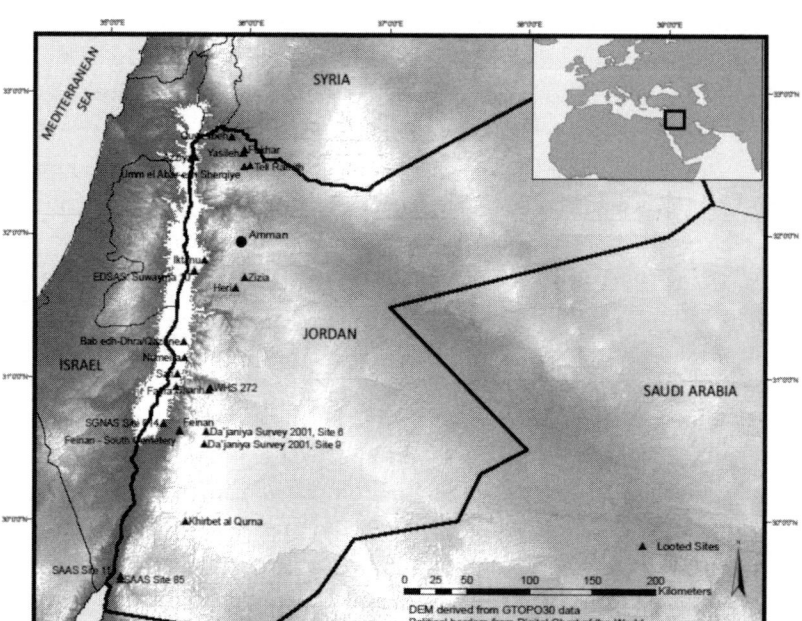

Figure 2. Map of Jordan showing places mentioned in the text.

the 1960s by Paul Lapp (Lapp 1966; Schaub and Rast 1989), who was drawn there by the large quantities of EBA pottery appearing in the antiquities shops of Jerusalem and Amman and rumors that the Bâb edh-Dhrâ' cemetery was a major source (Lapp 1966:104; McCreery 1996:5). During a preliminary visit to the site in 1964, Lapp was able to collect 60 more-or-less complete pots from the ground surface, although when he returned to excavate there in March 1965 he had difficulty at first in locating the cemetery area. It was not until a "local expert" alerted him to the surface indications of tombs that he was able to start work (Lapp 1966:105). Lapp's difficulty in locating the cemetery suggests that at the time it was not pock-marked as it is today by the open mouths of looted tombs, and although some tombs must have been looted, as recounted by Lapp's "local expert," the number could not have been large.

Lapp went on to excavate 53 EBA tombs, which were spatially clustered in two areas that he designated as Cemetery A on the east of the site and the smaller Cemetery C to the northwest (Figure 3) (Schaub and Rast 1989:25). Most of the excavated tombs were Early Bronze IA shaft

Figure 3. Google Earth image of the looted cemetery of Bâb edh-Dhrâ. Looted areas are outlined in white. The locations of graves excavated during formal projects are marked by black dots.

tombs (33 in total), each tomb comprising one or more burial chambers dug out radially from the bottom of an axial shaft (Schaub and Rast 1989:35–318). For the 33 tombs, 53 burial chambers were excavated, each one containing multiple inhumation burials and associated artifacts. Evidence of illegal digging was noted for eight tombs, but only one tomb (A84) seems to have been badly damaged. The second most frequent tomb type was the EB II-III charnel house. Eight charnel houses were excavated, with a ninth dating to EB IB (Schaub and Rast 1989: 319–472). Again, the charnel houses contained multiple inhumations with associated artifacts.

Excavations resumed in 1975. Over four seasons (1975, 1977, 1979, and 1981), a further 27 EB IA shaft tombs were excavated, comprising 63 burial chambers (Schaub 2008). Most chambers appeared to be have been undisturbed by looting, although two had been robbed out, and surface indications of several more robbed tombs were noted in Area G. A further three charnel houses were excavated.

Into the early 1980s, then, it was still possible to locate many undisturbed tombs, and although evidence of tomb robbing was noted, the cemetery appears to have been largely intact. By the mid-1990s, however, the situation had clearly deteriorated. A short rescue excavation conducted there in 1995 investigated 39 previously unrecorded EB IA shaft tombs clustered in a small area of the cemetery, comprising 64 chambers, that had been uncovered by illicit digging (McCreery 1996). In the limited time available it was not possible to clear all the tombs and inventory their contents, but the statistics from unsilted (and therefore intact) chambers are suggestive. Of the 44 chambers investigated that had been looted, only 20 yielded whole or restorable pots; the remaining 20 chambers had clearly been emptied of their contents.

The artifact assemblage recovered from the EB IA shaft tombs comprises mainly pottery, with a small number of stone objects (maceheads and basalt bowls), beads, and objects made of organic materials such as wood and leather. From the 53 chambers opened by Lapp, for example, there were 1182 pots, 41 stone bowls and maceheads, and 17 beads (Schaub and Rast 1989: x, Table 5; 203, Table 8). Similar quantities and proportions were recovered in the 1975–1981 excavation campaign (Schaub 2008:28, Table 4.1; 29, Tables 4.2–4.4). Thus, the saleable assemblage from these tombs is comprised overwhelmingly of pottery. A similar assemblage of artifacts was recovered from the EB II-III tombs. Typologically, the EB IA and EB II-III ceramic assemblages resemble one another, comprising mainly undecorated bowls and jars/juglets in a range of different sizes, although the EB IA types are on average larger (Schaub and Rast 1989:249, Figure 148; 419, Figure 251; 421–422, Figures 252 and 253, 423). This size difference might have important implications for marketability, which are discussed further below.

In 2008, we used Quickbird imagery available on Google Earth to estimate the total looted area at Bâb edh-Dhrâ' to be 74,377m^2 (Figures 3, 4) (Contreras and Brodie 2010). We used this figure in conjunction with information derived from the excavation reports to estimate the total number of tombs in the looted area and the quantity of pottery that might have been acquired from the total number of these tombs, assuming them all to have been looted. Documented excavations had shown that the incidence of burial chambers and the quantities of their offerings are not constant across the site, as the mean number of chambers per tomb and the mean number of pots per chamber were both lower for Cemetery C than for Cemetery A. Thus, we calculated two estimates of looted pottery, a low estimate based on the Cemetery C statistics, and a high estimate based on the Cemetery A statistics. The true figure would lie somewhere in between. The low damage estimate was that 669 chambers had been looted and 9,366 pots removed. The high damage estimate was that 1,190 chambers had been looted and 28,084 pots removed. These estimates of

The Economics of the Looted Archaeological Site of Bâb edh-Dhrâ'   19

Figure 4. The surface of Bab edh-Dhra in 2009 pock-marked by looters' pits (photograph D. Contreras).

the amounts of pottery that have been looted from Bâb edh-Dhrâ' seem unusually high, and the high estimate in particular looks questionable, but they are not totally unrealistic. Although there is no reason to believe that rich Cemetery A–type tombs were found across the whole cemetery area, and that Cemetery C–types might have been more widespread than is evident from excavated areas, Cemetery A–types are found at higher elevations (McCreery 1996:57), and it is mainly the higher elevation areas that are looted. There is no guarantee, either, that all the looting pits visible on Google Earth penetrated burial chambers or that all chambers in the looted area have been looted. Many chambers will have collapsed since the Bronze Age. Nevertheless, we are confident that, in general, the densely pitted areas do represent evidence of looting. It is hard to believe that diggers would persevere in that way if there were no tombs to find, particularly if they had recourse to long probing rods for locating burial chambers. This technique seems attested by the fact that some looted chambers had been entered directly through the roof and not by means of the adjoining shaft (McCreery 1996:53). (The fact that diggers are knowledgeable about site locations has been noted before. In Peru's Virú Valley, for example, many previously unknown sites have been discovered by undocumented digging [Contreras 2010].) In any case, as we examine

The London Market for Jordanian EBA Pottery

By the mid-1990s, it was easy to buy Jordanian EB IA pottery—generally described as "Old Testament"—in London. Round-bottomed juglets were being offered for between £45–50 each, depending on size, and bowls for between £70–175 (Martin 1996:8). Surprisingly, perhaps, there was no obvious EB II-III pottery for sale, as might have been expected had Bâb edh-Dhrâ' been a source. Perhaps the EB II-III pottery was in a poorer state of preservation than EB IA and, thus, less marketable. A large part of the EB II-III pottery found during formal excavations was in burnt destruction deposits, and although much was clearly fragmentary, more than 450 whole vessels were recovered. Perhaps even whole vessels from those burnt deposits would have been too badly damaged by burning to be marketable, although the crucial impediment to their sale is most likely size. Illustrations of whole pots found in EB II-III charnel houses show the predominant forms to have been small juglets, 10 cm or less high, and small bowls, also less than 10 cm high and 15 cm in diameter. Equivalent EB IA pots were usually larger, as were the EB IA pots on sale in London. The smallest EB IA juglets on offer in London were 10 cm high, and the smallest EB IA bowls were 18 cm in diameter (Martin 1996:8). The prices of the EB IA pots were directly related to their size, so perhaps simply, it was not sufficiently profitable to trade in small objects, and thus, EB II-III pots were not considered marketable.

The EB IA pottery achieved minor celebrity in 1996 when it was featured in a two-page color spread in the "Homes & Gardens" section of the *Guardian Weekend* magazine (Murphy 1996). The article was advertizing the then-innovative marketing strategy, adopted by London dealer Chris Martin, of selling antiquities by mail order. It prompted an angry response from British Museum archaeologist Konstantinos D. Politis, who claimed that the material was coming from robbed cemeteries in Jordan. At the time Politis was excavating the badly looted EBA cemetery at an-Naq' (Politis 2002:Figures 14.6, 14.7). Martin claimed in his defense that his pottery did not come from an-Naq', that he had bought it in London from a Jordanian citizen, and that it had been part of a consignment exported from Jordan in 1988 with appropriate legal documentation (Newnham 1996:72). This documentation includes an English language translation of a Jordanian export license, which purports to authorize the legal export of 2000 ceramic objects. The number quoted on the license gives some idea of the quantities of pottery that were being exported at the time, and more consignments followed (Newnham 1996:72). Furthermore, although Martin obtained his stock in London, he clearly knew something about the size of the cemetery at Bâb edh-Dhrâ' and that it was capable of disgorging an exceedingly large number of pots, as he made the unlikely suggestion that there were between 10 and 15 million pots still in the ground there. Against Martin's guess of millions, even our high damage estimate of 28,084 pots begins to look like a conservative one.

There were still a large number of EB IA antiquities for sale on the Internet in August 2008, and prices had climbed appreciably. Martin's present company Ancient and Oriental was offering a bowl for £200 (22 cm diameter, a bowl this size would have been offered for £135 in the late 1990s) and a one-handled juglet, said to come from "Transjordan," for £150 (14 cm high; a juglet this size would have been offered for £50 in the late 1990s).[2] Another Web site was offering a bowl for £210, accompanied by the provenance ex-Peter Negus collection, and said to be from Bâb edh-Dhrâ', in "southern Palestine."[3] At first sight, the mention of Bâb edh-Dhrâ' in a statement of provenance appears surprising, bordering on a tacit admission that the artifact had first been obtained in illegal circumstances. But it is less surprising when it is remembered that dealers are more concerned about assuring their customers of authenticity than legal export (Tubb and Brodie 2001:108–110). Thanks to the legitimate excavations of the 1960s and 1970s and their exemplary publication, Bâb edh-Dhrâ' is now a "known site" that exists in the literature. By associating a pot with a known site, the dealer is able to increase its historical interest and reassure potential customers about authenticity. By the same token, it is interesting to note that many pots offered for sale on the Internet are said to be from the area of Jericho, another known (and famous) site. Whether or not such pots actually do derive from their attributed sites is open to speculation.

Discussion

It is possible to combine information obtained from Google Earth, published excavation reports, sales catalogs, and media reporting to make some inferences about the economics of looting at Bâb edh-Dhrâ' that might stand comparison to Rose and Burke's (2004) figures. According to Politis, who conducted extensive interviews in the area of an-Naq' in the late 1990s, about 20 km away from Bâb edh-Dhrâ' (Politis 2002: 263), local people digging up tombs were being paid something like one pound (British) for four pots, when the average daily wage was the equivalent of three pounds (British) per day (Newnham 1996:71). At that time, as noted above, pots were being sold in London for prices in the range £70–175 (say, £122 each). If these figures are applied to the Bâb edh-Dhrâ' damage estimates, then for the low damage estimate of 9,366 pots, the people digging and selling them would have received a total sum of something in the region of £2,342 over a period of several years. On the London market the same pots would have sold for £1,142,652. For the high damage estimate of 28,084 pots, the diggers would have received £7,021, and the pots would have sold in London for £3,426,248.

The estimated £2,342 to £7,021 (between $3,864 and $11,585 at late 1990s exchange rates) revenue of sold pots from Bâb edh-Dhrâ' stands comparison to Rose and Burke's (2004) conclusion that each cemetery in their study area had the potential to generate between $13,000 and $24,000 through sale of their artifacts. (A small amount of extra money would have been available from Bâb edh-Dhrâ' from the sale of other artifacts.) It is important to point out, however, that there are some important discrepancies in the underlying data. Rose and Burke (2004) reported for their study area that diggers were receiving something like $7–15 each for artifacts (estimated above to be about 15 percent final sale price), whereas Politis reported a much lower figure of less than a dollar a pot (about 0.2 percent final sale price). When compared to the 1 percent norm derived from data in Table 1, Politis's figure of one pound (British) for four pots in the Ghor es-Safi area looks suspiciously low, whereas Rose and Burke's figure of $7–15 per artifact looks suspiciously high. Perhaps the investigators have misreported or been misinformed, but that is not necessarily the case. The conditions and availability of paid employment in the Ghor es-Safi might be poorer than those in Irbid, and thus more conducive to digging for lower rewards. Another reason for lower prices in the Ghor es-Safi might be that whereas Bâb edh-Dhrâ' was giving up its thousands of pots, the nearby EBA cemeteries of Fayfa' and an-Naq' were also being looted. There was a potential output from these three cemeteries of tens of thousands of pots, and there was no evidence on the market of anything like that number. Perhaps, in this case, prices on the ground were responding to broader market conditions and were being driven down by oversupply.

It is too soon to draw any firm socioeconomic conclusions from these data, but it is worthwhile trying to develop some macroeconomic contexts. The cemeteries of Bâb edh-Dhrâ', Fayfa', and an-Naq' are located in the Karak administrative area, which in 2003 had a population of 214,225.[4] As it stands at the moment, if we hypothesize that each of the cemeteries had a commodity value of something in the region of $8,000, the sale on the ground of the total contents of all three cemeteries would have generated about four cents per inhabitant of the Karak area. Even if other large looted cemeteries in the region, such as the Nabataean one of Qazone, are added to the equation, we would be struggling to suggest that on average, the sale of the contents of all tombs would have generated more than one dollar per inhabitant. Rose and Burke's (2004) study was conducted in the more fertile and, thus, more populous administrative region of Irbid. They estimated a total commodity value for all 745 known Roman-Byzantine cemeteries of between $10 to $18 million. In 2003, the population of the Irbid region was 950,695, so that revenue would have broken down to between $10 and $18 per inhabitant. These per capita figures are total, not annual, and suggest that, overall, subsistence digging/looting does not make a large contribution to the regional economies of Jordan—certainly nothing comparable to the annual $1,000 per person reported by Hollowell for St. Lawrence Island. Clearly, however, not everyone is engaged in digging, and the money made by the probably small number of people who are would be more than the averages estimated here. Nevertheless, if the general public is not benefiting monetarily to any great extent, it suggests that financially modest strategies of heritage management aimed at emphasizing the potential of heritage as an educational resource or a tourist attraction might enjoy some measure of public support, mobilized to discourage digging through ostracism or other means of social persuasion. Of course, the effectiveness of social persuasion would further depend on the extent to which the digging is criminally organized and officially ignored or condoned. It is a matter of some urgency that accurate and verifiable information about prices on the ground, the factors involved in their formation, their economic outcomes, and the organization of the local market should be collected in Jordan and in other areas to build on the arguments offered here and to make more concrete suggestions.

Acknowledgments. This work was made possible by the support of the British Academy, the Stanford Archaeology Center, and especially by the generous donation of David Sherman.

Notes

1. Except, occasionally, legacy laws such as the United Kingdom's Treasure Act incorporates a monetary rewards system based on the commodity values of found artifacts.

2. http://www.antiquities.co.uk/.

3. http://www.ancientrelics.co.uk/ANE_NEW_Page8.htm.

4. Data obtained from the Hashemite Kingdom of Jordan Department of Statistics at http://www.dos.gov.jo/dos_home/dos_home_e/main/index.htm.

3

The Material and Intellectual Consequences of Acquiring the Sarpedon Krater

DAVID GILL

The return of the Sarpedon krater to Italy in 2008 has highlighted a number of issues about the acquisition of recently surfacing antiquities, the destruction of the archaeological record, and the intellectual consequences of the loss of knowledge. Discussions about looted antiquities tend to focus on the material consequences: destroyed cemeteries and disturbed occupation layers. There are more serious intellectual consequences: the loss of knowledge and the creation of possibly flawed theories and approaches that try to reclaim what has gone forever (Gill and Chippindale 1993). The centerpiece of this study is a figure-decorated clay pot made at Athens in the late sixth century B.C.

The loss of context is not unusual for objects that surface on the market. Among the 130 or so objects returned to Italy in the last few years there are 34 Athenian pots: six from Boston's Museum of Fine Arts (Gill and Chippindale 2006:324–325, nos. 3–8), 17 from the J. Paul Getty Museum (Gill and Chippindale 2007a:228–229, nos. 7–15; Gill 2010b:105–06, nos. 1–3, 10–14), two additional pieces from New York's Metropolitan Museum of Art (Gill 2010b:106, nos. 3–4), one from the Princeton University Art Museum (Gill 2010b:106–107, no. 3), one from the Minneapolis Institute of Arts, three from the Royal-Athena Galleries in New York (Gill 2010b:107, nos. 1–3), and four from the Shelby White collection (Gill 2010b:108, nos. 2–5). Virtually nothing is known about their final resting-places and the associated material. A cup signed by Euphronios and attributed to Onesimos was returned to Italy from the J. Paul Getty Museum in 1999 (Sgubini 1999; see also Williams 1991).

25

The inscribed Etruscan dedication pointed it to a sanctuary of Ercle at Cerveteri (Heurgon 1989; Silver 2009:166–168).

The passion to acquire figure-decorated Athenian pottery can be traced back to at least the late eighteenth century. One stimulus was the selling of the collection of Sir William Hamilton formed from explorations in the cemeteries around the Bay of Naples during the Napoleonic Wars (Jenkins and Sloan 1996). Part of this collection was dispersed at the Hope sale in 1917 and entered several public collections (Tillyard 1923). The rise of connoisseurship for the study of Greek figure-decorated pottery led to it being viewed as high art (Kurtz 1989). Museum directors now consider it appropriate to acquire recently surfaced antiquities in order, as they would see it, to "preserve" the objects (Cuno 2005:155), though there are concerns that it is the collecting process that encourages looting (Gill 2009a).

History of Acquisition

The recent history of the Sarpedon krater has been well rehearsed (Silver 2009). The Athenian red-figured calyx-krater was acquired by the Metropolitan Museum of Art in November 1972 for US $1 million (Bothmer 1987; Silver 2009:50–75). It appears that it was brought to the MMA's attention by Robert E. Hecht Jr. in February of that year (Silver 2009:53; Watson and Todeschini 2006:x). Thomas Hoving, the director of the MMA, and Dietrich von Bothmer, the curator of the Greek and Roman Department, saw it in Zurich in June, apparently in the workshop of Fritz Bürki (Silver 2009:65–66; Watson and Todeschini 2006: xiii, 187). It was transported to New York in August (Silver 2009:69).

Nicholas Gage followed the trail of the Sarpedon krater back to Zurich and Rome, receiving the report that it "had been dug up in late 1971 in a necropolis north of Rome" and sold to Hecht for US $100,000 (Watson and Todeschini 2006:xii). Further enquiries took him to the Cerveteri home of a *tomborolo*, Armando Cenere, who admitted that he had dug up the krater at Sant'Angelo in November 1971 (Silver 2009:92; Watson and Todeschini 2006:xiv).

A false trail leading to Dikran A. Sarrafian of Beirut had also been laid (Watson and Todeschini 2006:xii); it was even suggested that the krater had been acquired in London in 1920. It now seems that the fragments in the possession of Sarrafian formed the krater that passed into the Hunt collection and subsequently Shelby White and Leon Levy (Silver 2009:136–137; Watson and Todeschini 2006:169–170).

The link between the krater and Giacomo Medici were confirmed when photographs of Medici, posing by the krater in the MMA, were seized (Silver 2009:ill; Watson and Todeschini 2006:107, 2000–2002).

The Lost Archaeological Context

There is no confirmed or documented information about the find-spot of the Sarpedon krater. Can we be sure that the krater was found in Etruria? Was it Cerveteri? Which cemetery? Which grave? Where was it placed in the tomb? What was the status of the person buried in the tomb? What was the date of the burial? What other objects were placed alongside the krater? How does the iconography of "Sleep" and "Death" on the krater link to the iconography of other funerary objects from the same tomb?

This is not the only calyx-krater attributed to Euphronios that has lost its context in recent years. There is the fragmentary example acquired by Shelby White and Leon Levy (Gill 2010b:108), and four fragments from another acquired by Princeton University Art Museum in 1997 (Padgett 2001; Princeton 1997:488a–d). The Princeton fragments are reported to have been acquired from Princeton alumnus, Edoardo Almagià (Eakin and Povoledo 2010).

Find-Spots for Euphronios

The find-spot for the Sarpedon krater is unknown although it has been suggested that it was removed from a tomb in one of the cemeteries of Cerveteri in Tuscany (Silver 2009:38–43, 271). The fact that the krater is nearly complete suggests that it came from a tomb; pots found on domestic sites are normally very fragmentary. A krater of this size would have been an unusual find at Athens, and it is likely that the krater was placed in a large tomb. A find-spot in Etruria is certainly plausible.

Calyx-kraters attributed to Euphronios have been found in Italy (see also Exhibition Catalogue 1990). Among them is the "signed" example from Cerveteri (Paris, Louvre, inv. G103) showing Herakles wrestling with Antaios, and a second is said to be from Capua in Campania (Berlin inv. F2180) that is decorated with athletic scenes. An amphora, attributed to Euphronios and showing a sympotic scene, is said to have been found at Vulci (Paris, Louvre inv. G30). Another piece from Vulci is a cup decorated on the outside with Herakles and the Nemean lion (Munich inv. 2620). A pelike found near Viterbo is now in the Villa Guilia in Rome. A fragment from a pelike in The David and Alfred Smart Gallery of the University of Chicago (inv. 1967.115.1; Moon and Berge 1980:136–137, no. 77) had once been in the Castellani collection and is said to have been found at Cerveteri; it comes from the same pelike as other fragments in the Villa Guilia. Another piece from Cerveteri is a psykter with a sympotic scene now in St Petersburg (inv. ST1670). Finally, a fragment of a calyx-krater showing a warrior was excavated at Gravisca and has been attributed to Euphronios. The find-spot of Cerveteri is inferred for the Euphronios-Onesimos cup returned from the J. Paul Getty Museum as the foot had a graffito showing it was dedicated to Ercle (Sgubini 1999). A further fragment of the cup was reported to have been found during a police raid at Cerveteri in 2008.

Given these stated find-spots for pots attributed to Euphronios, it is quite likely (though not certain) that the Sarpedon krater was found in Etruria. However, pieces are found further afield such as the fragment of a cup found at Olbia in southern Russia, that has been attributed to Euphronios (St Petersburg O18181). A fragmentary signed cup showing the wedding of Peleus and Thetis was found on the Athenian akropolis (Athens Acr. Mus. 15214).

One further modern aspect of this attribution of works "signed" by or attributed to Euphronios is that it has made some observe that such Athenian pots were intended to be exported. Indeed, it has been estimated that some 30,000 Greek pots have come from tombs in Etruria (Osborne 2001:277; see also Osborne 1996). Thus, their continuing movement into North American markets is seen by some as a natural progression (see de Montebello 2007:34). Such views are coming from those who wish to encourage a "licit market" in antiquities while ignoring the potential problems that this could have for the destruction of archaeological sites. In any case, there is a major difference between pots exported from Attica to Etruria (to be placed in a tomb), and pots looted from Etruscan cemeteries to supply the international market in antiquities.

Leagros kalos

The Sarpedon krater is normally dated to c. 515 B.C. How is that date obtained? The krater has to be placed in a stylistic sequence of early Athenian red-figured pottery. The "orthodox" view is that Euphronios was active as a pot-painter between 520 and 505 B.C. (Padgett 2001:12). Yet it is possible that although the krater was made in the late sixth century B.C., it was not placed in the tomb until the second quarter of the fifth century B.C. It could have been the cherished heirloom of an Etruscan family who retained it above ground.

Dyfri Williams has observed such a phenomenon in the composition of the Brygos Tomb from Campania (Williams 1992:632). There the Brygos cup and the Hieron skyphos may be dated ten to twenty years earlier than other material from the group. He suggested: "the two earlier pieces were either prized possessions of the deceased during his lifetime, being used and loved for many years before his death, or if he died young, they could have been inherited from his father." A similar phenomenon has been noted for the Blacas Tomb, also in Campania (Corbett 1960:59–60).

The separate piece of evidence is the painted inscription "Leagros kalos" on the krater; similar inscriptions are found on the kraters attributed to Euphronios from Cerveteri (Paris G103) and Capua (Berlin F2180). Such *kalos* ("fine," "beautiful") inscriptions are usually linked to the praise of adolescent males in Athenian society. Leagros is normally associated with the Athenian general of the same name who served in 465 B.C. As the Athenian democracy had set age limits on the holding of such an office, it is likely that Leagros was born between 525 and 495 B.C. (Francis and Vickers 1981; see also Cook 1989:167). In which case Leagros would have been called *kalos* (or "beautiful") in a period between 510 and 480 B.C. It is also worth making the point that the inscription, written for a specific Athenian male audience, would have been irrelevant in an Etruscan funerary context.

Interpreting the Iconography in an Etruscan Context

The calyx-krater was decorated with a dying warrior with blood gushing from his wounds lying on the field of battle; he is identified by an adjacent inscription as Sarpedon. On either side the winged figures of *Hypnos*

(Sleep) and *Thanatos* (Death) are preparing to lift him up. Behind the group is Hermes, the messenger of the gods.

This is a representation of the battle before Troy vividly described in the Homeric *Iliad* :

> but after the soul and the years of his life have left him, then send
> Death to carry him away, and Sleep, who is painless,
> until they come with him to the countryside of broad Lykia
> where his brothers and countrymen shall give him due burial
> with tomb and gravestone. Such is the privilege of those who have perished
> [Lattimore 1961:16.453–457].

This narrative imagery would have appealed to a Greek or Athenian audience familiar with the epic poem (Snodgrass 1998). But how would it have related to an Etruscan viewer (Gill and Vickers 1995)? Scenes from the Trojan War, except for Aias and Achilles, are rare on figure-decorated Etruscan pottery (Osborne 2001:287). Yet Hypnos and Thantos do appear on engraved Etruscan mirrors (Osborne 2001:285). Yet the image of a fallen hero from the Trojan War being escorted from the field of battle by the messenger of the gods and carried by the personification of Sleep and Death could have had appeal for a member of the Etruscan social elite. The image itself is also found on a cup "signed" by Euphronios and once in the collection of the Hunt brothers (Tompkins 1983:54–57, no. 5). This cup appears to have surfaced in Zurich in July 1971 and had once been in the possession of Hecht (Silver 2009:130–132; Watson and Todeschini 2006: xv–xvi). A red-figured calyx-krater attributed to the Eucharides painter and said to be from Cerveteri also shows the removal of Sarpeon's body by Sleep and Death (Paris, Louvre G163).

The krater is a vessel intended for the mixing of wine and water at the Greek symposium (Lissarague 1990:19–46). The presence in a funerary context suggests the importance of creating a dining setting for the deceased. Perhaps one of the most elaborate is the Tomb of the Reliefs at Cerveteri, which has carved couches for the diners complete with (stone) cushions (Blanck and Proietti 1986). Drinking cups and pieces of armour are "hung" on the walls. In other less-elaborate Etruscan tombs, kraters appear in the painted decoration.

High Art?

The Sarpedon krater was the first piece of Athenian pottery to fetch a price of US $1 million. The attribution of figure-decorated pottery to named or anonymous painters goes back to the nineteenth century (Rouet 2001). Scholars recognized some pots carried painted inscriptions giving a personal name with the verb *egraphsen* or *epoiesen*, and these were interpreted as either the painter or potter (but see Vickers and Gill 1994:154–168). In the case of the Sarpedon krater, where such inscriptions are found, the traditional interpretation is that Euphronios was the pot-painter and Euxitheos was the potter. This scholarship developed the theory that Athenian pottery was highly prized in antiquity and that potters and pot-painters had a high status in Athenian society.

Yet it is now clear that the evidence of inscribed monumental dedications from the Athenian acropolis was far from secure and open to alternative interpretations (Vickers and Gill 1994). Moreover, the evidence from commercial graffiti provides prices for Athenian pottery (e.g., Gill 1991, 1994, 1998; Johnston 2006). Thus, a batch of four pots attributed to the Achilles painter was valued at 3 1/2 obols (there were six obols to a silver Athenian drachma, weighing 4.31 g). It is rare for pots to be valued at more than a drachma: two kraters from sites on Sicily carried price inscriptions of 10 and 9 obols. Yet at the same time a silver phiale, with gold-figured decoration, from a Thracian tomb at Duvanli (in modern Bulgaria) weighed the equivalent of 100 drachmas (or 1 mina). These ancient values, where gold and silver plate was valued, have been inverted so that a more humble medium is seen to be an example of "high art." This is reinforced when figure-decorated pottery is displayed in the same institution as paintings by Titian, El Greco, Peter Paul Rubens, Rembrandt, and Paul Cézanne. It is perhaps significant that Thomas Hoving, the director responsible for the acquisition of the Sarpedon krater, called it "the single most perfect work of art I had ever encountered" (quoted in Mead 2007:54).

Apart from the inscription identifying Euphronios as the "painter," there is a second painted inscription giving the name of Euxitheos as the "potter." There are at least four other known instances of this inscription. A second calyx-krater, attributed to Euphronios, is decorated with Dionysos and the Maenads (Paris, Louvre G33); like the Sarpedon krater it also has a *Leagros kalos* inscription. Two cups "potted" by Euxitheos are also "signed" by Oltos as painter: one said to have been found at Vulci shows the fight over the dead Patroklos (Berlin F2264), and the other found at Tarquinia shows the Olympian gods (Tarquinia RC6848). The final piece is an amphora, reported to have been found at Vulci and attributed to (but not "signed" by) Oltos (London, British Museum E258).

This has brought about a modern emphasis on the creator of the pot at the expense of its ancient context. Thus John Boardman (2006:39) in commenting on the Sarpedon krater could observe:

> the interest of which is 98 per cent in its sheer existence (we know who made it, when and where) with only a 2 per cent loss in knowledge of what Etruscan grave it came from.

Yet without the archaeological context and the information it could have provided, scholars dwell on the makers or decorators of the pot. Boardman's views are echoed by de Montebello who disputes the importance of archaeological context and suggests that general context can be reconstructed from "intrinsic qualities" (de Montebello 2007:34).

Philippe de Montebello on the Sarpedon Krater

Philippe de Montebello, the outgoing director of the MMA, has commented on the return of the Sarpedon krater in several places. One of his fullest comments was in his 2007 Stephen Kellen Lecture given at the American Academy in Berlin (de Montebello 2007). He posed the question, "Who Owns Culture?" and presented the area as "a highly controversial issue, surrounded by a considerable degree of exaggeration, misunderstanding and 'political correctness'" (de Montebello 2007:33). Yet the issue is as much about the stewardship of the archaeological record in Italy than the right of public museums and private collectors to "own" cultural artifacts.

There is a growing understanding from de Montebello that the archaeological concern over the acquisition of recently surfaced antiquities has been over the destruction of previously unrecorded (and unexcavated) archaeological sites. Yet it is not possible to agree entirely with his view that "ours is an era of ... scrupulous acquisition policies" (de Montebello 2007:34). Why have six prestigious North American museums that are members of the Association of Art Museum Directors (AAMD) been able to acquire antiquities that they have agreed to return? Taking the returns to Italy from the Cleveland Museum of Art, the Getty, MFA, MMA, and Princeton, over 27 percent of the objects (30 out of 111 items) were acquired in the 1990s (Gill 2009a:82, fig. 1). This perhaps suggests that museum curatorial staff have chosen to ignore concerns from the archaeological community in their pursuit of stunning acquisitions. And these flawed acquisition policies have seen museums returning ten of millions of dollars worth of antiquities to Italy.

De Montebello rightly emphasizes the movement of objects in antiquity and cites examples from Pompeii and Gandhara. I have discussed with Christopher Chippindale a Roman silver cup in an anonymous North American private collection ("AIC") that is said to come from Gandhara (Chippindale and Gill 2000:489–490). But the find-spot is not certain. The cup comes from a collection with an emphasis on Gandhara; would a buyer sell it with an appropriate "find-spot"? There is a huge difference between "excavated at" and "said to be from"; there are intellectual consequences for the study of the discipline. Has de Montebello understood the issues? He even makes the outrageous suggestion that archaeologists are to blame for the loss of information because dealers who handle "illegitimate objects" (de Montebello 2007:35) do not say where it was found for fear of prosecution. There is not a hint that the fault could lie with the looters, dealers, or indeed the end-of-line institutions.

De Montebello makes the point that few antiquities in museums "have a known find spot or clear archaeological provenance" (de Montebello 2007:35). Indeed he suggested in the 2006 debate following the announced return of the krater:

> I think the reality, since we have been talking about the Euphronios vase, is that the knowledge that we have of Greek vase painting is based 98 percent on vases that were never excavated by licensed archaeologists. Archaeologists talk about the loss of context. We have almost a totality of the possible knowledge we could have, although we don't know what the vase painters ate.

Is he suggesting that only some 2 percent of Greek pottery have been properly and scientifically excavated? This is probably too low, and figures for Athenian red-figured pots attributed to the Berlin painter suggest a figure close to 13 percent (Gill 2003, 2009a:98). While it is possible to gain some information from the krater itself (de Montebello 2009:65), it is hard to avoid the conclusion that the loss of context has had wider consequences. It is also important to stress that the loss of archaeological information does not necessarily mean "stolen." De Montebello has suggested, in a tongue-in-cheek fashion, that "by today's standards, all of the works in the Vatican are stolen" (de Montebello 2007:35). Athenian figure-decorated pots removed from Etruscan tombs on estates belonging to the Vatican at least are known to come from Etruria. But how certain can we be that the Euphronios krater was found in a grave in Tuscany?

Loot is a major theme for de Montebello. And certainly spoils were removed from sites in antiquity. For example, a silver phiale dedicated in a sanctuary at Megara has turned up in a late classical tomb at Kozani in Macedonia (Gill 1990). And de Montebello points to Roman "trophies of conquest." But we could continue to more modern trophies of war such as the hoards from Troy removed from Berlin at the end of the Second World War (Antonova et al. 1996). But relatively recent wartime looting from museums and archaeological stores is different to the deliberate destruction of archaeological contexts to provide new acquisitions for museums remote from the country where the pieces were found.

De Montebello makes an important point about separating finds. He cites the way that the Nimrud Ivories were divided between three collections. This he claims preserved part of the collection when the pieces in Baghdad were damaged during the First Gulf War and the later looting of the Baghdad Museum. But spreading scientifically excavated material between different collections, *partage*, is different to displaying pots excavated in the cemeteries of Cerveteri in the Villa Guilia and ones that have no recorded find-spot (and are presumably looted) in a public collection in North America.

De Montebello also considers the implication of the Frederick Schultz case and suggests that it is "one of the reasons why countries like Greece, Turkey, and especially Italy are now making claims against US institutions" (de Montebello 2007:36). He grumbles that European museums also collected from "now discredited dealers like Robin Symes and Robert Hecht ... but for the moment seem to be inviolate" (de Montebello 2007:36). While that is true, Italy has indicated that it wishes to discuss the return of antiquities from the Ny Carlsberg in Copenhagen, and an unsuccessful attempt was made to return a piece of armor (probably found in Apulia) from Leiden that had surfaced on the antiquities market in 1997.

De Montebello also notes the implication of the "Medici Conspiracy" (Watson and Todeschini 2006; see also Gill and Chippindale 2007b) and the evidence of the Polaroids "showing clear evidence that objects had been stolen in modern times" (de Montebello 2007:36). He goes on to mention the MMA's return of the Euphronios krater and the "Morgantina" silver. It should be noted that he uses the word "stolen" to describe the "looting" of ancient cemeteries. Yet "stealing" implies "theft" of objects "owned" by another, and the use of such language by de Montebello reflects his interest in "ownership" than cultural protection. This is reflected in his closing appeal: "As the philosopher Kwame Anthony Appiah has argued, the treasures in the world's major museums belong to an international, cosmopolitan society" (de Montebello 2007:37; see Appiah 2006).

The issue of historic collections is addressed sensibly by de Montebello. A distinction needs to be made between cases of recent looting and historic claims over cultural property that was removed from their country of origin decades, if not centuries, before. He cites the head of Nefertiti, the Pergamon altar, and the Parthenon marbles. He reminds us that pieces can have different settings: the horses of San Marco have contexts in Constantinople, Venice, and Paris. One could also draw attention to the way that in Late Antiquity the snake tripod marking the end of the Persian Wars was moved from Delphi to Constantinople; it is still visible in the hippodrome in Istanbul. Or indeed the colossal chryselephantine statue of Zeus from Olympia was moved to Constantinople and destroyed in a fire. However, de Montebello makes a great leap when he suggests "we should recognize that a great deal of knowledge, cross-fertilization, and exchange can come from objects moving across borders" (de Montebello 2007:37). It is almost as if he is saying that it is a good thing for, say, an Attic red-figured krater to move across international frontiers from Italy to the USA (and that we can ignore the resulting loss of knowledge).

A Motif for Recently Surfaced Antiquities

The acquisition of the Sarpedon krater raised the awareness of the issue of recently surfaced antiquities in the immediate aftermath of the 1970 UNESCO Convention on the Means of Prohibiting and Preventing the Illicit Import, Export and Transfer of Ownership of Cultural Property. This coincided with the Archaeological Institute of America's (AIA) 1970 resolution:

> The Archaeological Institute of America calls upon its members, as well as educational institutions (universities and museums) in the United States and Canada, to refrain from purchasing and accepting donations of antiquities exported from their countries of origin in contravention to the terms of the UNESCO Draft Convention.

Indeed, it could be argued that the actions of the MMA were the final catalysts for the December 1973 Archaeological Institute of America's resolution that included (see also Silver 2009:76–79):

> The Archaeological Institute of America believes that Museums can henceforth best implement such cooperation by refusing to acquire through purchase, gift, or bequest cultural property exported subsequent to December 30, 1973, in violation of the laws obtaining in the countries of origin.

After 1973, archaeologists and museum professionals in North America (and beyond) were well aware of the issues surrounding the looting of archaeological sites. Indeed, one of the markers that can be used for working out the patterns for acquisitions has been 1973 (e.g., Chippindale and Gill 2000; Chippindale et al. 2001). Even so, one prominent New York collector, Shelby White, suggested that awareness of the problem of looted antiquities is recent: "It is hard to apply current standards to something that happened thirty years ago" (Mead 2007:60). Yet 30 years prior to this statement was 1977, four years after the AIA passed its resolution.

The date of the 1970 UNESCO Convention has clearly been sufficient in persuading North American museums to return antiquities. The earliest object returned from Boston to Italy, a Lucanian nestoris, was acquired in 1971 (Gill and Chippindale 2006). Likewise, the Roman fresco fragments were purchased by the J. Paul Getty Museum in 1971

(Gill and Chippindale 2007a). Moreover, the date of the 1970 UNESCO Convention was adopted in the 2006 guidelines on the accepting the loan of archaeological material by the Association of Art Museum Directors (AAMD).

In spite of this there has been a move to suggest that 1983, the year that the US Congress adopted the 1970 UNESCO convention, should be used as the cut off point. One of the most prominent people to call for the use of the later date has been James Cuno. He suggested that the adoption of the Convention had been taken:

> to enforce foreign nations' retentionist cultural policies at the expense of the Enlightenment principles on which public museums in the United States were established [Cuno 2005:144].

This proposal is presented as if it was unenlightened to be concerned about the destruction of archaeological sites or the conservation of finite cultural resources. It is the unreformed views of some museum directors and curatorial staff that has created the environment in which recently surfaced antiquities were acquired.

The adoption of 1983 would have excluded 22 pieces from the negotiated returns from Boston, Cleveland and Malibu, as well as part of the "Morgantina silver hoard" and the Sarpedon krater from the MMA.

One of the concerns for archaeologists is that looting destroys contexts. And once the destruction occurs no amount of scholarship can restore the information. At one level displaying an Attic krater in New York or Rome will make no difference to the lost archaeological context. However, the fact that a new acquisition could be swiftly deaccessioned and then returned to its country of origin is probably enough to make a curator think twice before acquiring it in the first place. Yet Cuno, the North American museum director, sees museums as places that will serve as the resting place for such newly surfaced antiquities:

> But when an antiquity is offered to a museum for acquisition, the looting, if indeed there was any, has already occurred. Now the museum must decide whether to bring the object into its public collection, where it can be preserved, studied, and enjoyed, and where its whereabouts can be made widely known. Museums are

havens for objects that are already, and for whatever reason, alienated from their original context [Cuno 2005:155].

Does acquiring looted material only encourage further looting?

One example of this is the way that thousands of previously unknown Apulian pots surfaced at auction through the 1980s and 1990s (Elia 2001). Their appearance is directly linked to the deliberate destruction of funerary contexts in southern Italy to supply a market. And the buyers have been public institutions and private collectors. So it does matter if there is active acquisition of Apulian pots because there is a material implication for the funerary record and an intellectual implication for their interpretation. Indeed, there is a further implication for the study of other material from the same graves. These include sets of armor for Italian cavalrymen that are in Boston (MFA 2003.815.1–4; first surfaced on the Köln market in 1975) and the Shelby White collection (e.g., David Cahn in Bothmer 1990:114–22, no. 95, "Set of armor from a burial"). This type of material is dated from tomb-groups that contained "Apulian red-figured vases, for which we have an established chronology" (David Cahn in Bothmer 1990:114).

Discouraging the acquisition of Apulian pottery unknown prior to 1970 is one way to discourage looting. The pieces of Apulian pottery attributed to the Darius painter and returned to Italy from Boston, Cleveland, Malibu, Princeton, as well as New York, have lost their contexts (Gill 2009a:79–80; see also Gill and Chippindale 2008); but their transfer of ownership will probably make those museums think twice about acquiring newly surfaced material. In all, 18 Apulian pots have been returned to Italy: three from Boston, five from Cleveland, seven from the Getty, one from the MMA, and two from Princeton (Gill and Chippindale 2006, 2007; Gill 2010b).

A further issue that is emerging from a study of the returned objects to Italy is that some names appear on a regular basis: Giacomo Medici, Fritz Bürki, Robert Hecht, and Atlantis Antiquities. This is likely to be more than a coincidence and suggests a systematic pillaging of our cosmopolitan and cultural heritage to feed the desires of unenlightened acquiring institutions. It is naïve to suggest that most antiquities appear on the market as a result of chance finds.

Yet it is important that while 1970 (or 1973) can be used as convenient markers for a change in professional and public attitudes towards looting, many countries have laws relating to antiquities that predate this. Thus, Turkey was able to mount a successful legal challenge to claim the major hoard of archaic silver from Lydia (Özgen and Öztürk 1996; see also Bothmer 1984). Greece has challenged the selling of fragments of Cycladic marble figurines as they were associated with the notorious Keros "haul" (Sotirakopoulou 2005; see also Gill 2007a).

A Motif for Repatriation: "*Successo storico*"

The Sarpedon krater was returned to Italy in 2008. It went on display in Rome on January 18, 2008. This "successo storico," as it was hailed in the Italian press, was the culmination of intense negotiations by Francesco Rutelli, the then Italian Minister of Culture. The return coincided with the display of antiquities from other largely North American collections in the Palazzo del Quirinale, Rome. The exhibition, "Nostoi: Capolavori Ritrovati," alluded to the Homeric return of Odysseus to Ithaca after the Trojan Wars (Gill 2009b). The exhibition included four other pieces from the Metropolitan Museum of Art: a Laconian cup with warrior attributed to the Hunt painter; an Attic red-figured psykter with young horseman attributed by Robert Guy to Smikros (once in the collection of Mr & Mrs Spears, Riverdale [NY]); an Attic red-figured amphora with Cithara player attributed to the Berlin painter; and an Apulian red-figured dinos with Herakles and Busiris attributed to the Darius painter. All four of these pieces apparently featured in the Polaroids seized in the Geneva Freeport (Watson and Todeshini 2006:106–108). Other sources for material included in "Nostoi" had been returned from the Museum of Fine Arts in Boston, the J. Paul Getty Museum, and the Princeton University Art Museum, as well as the Royal-Athena Galleries, New York, and Robin Symes.

The "Nostoi" exhibition was transferred to the Palazzo Poli in a slightly changed display; the Sarpedon krater joined an exhibition in Mantua along with two pieces returned from the J. Paul Getty Museum. In March 2008 the pieces in Rome were joined by part of the Shelby White collection; seven of the pieces had previously formed part of the "Glories of the Past" exhibition at the Metropolitan Museum of Art (Bothmer 1990). The tenth piece that will return later (2010) is a fragmentary Attic red-figured calyx-krater, "signed" by Euphronios showing Herakles slaying Kyknos (Boardman 2001:fig. 120). Like the one returned from the MMA it carried a "Leagros kalos" inscription. This second Euphronios krater featured in the Polaroids seized from Medici's premises in Geneva; the krater itself was "dirty and in separate fragments" (Watson and Todeschini 2006:128–132). It apparently had passed from Medici to Robert E. Hecht and thence to the Summa Gallery; it as purchased by the Hunt brothers, then sold at Sotheby's in New York (June 19, 1990) for US$ 1.76 million, and then purchased by Robin Symes on behalf of Leon Levy and Shelby White (Silver 2009:160–161, 201). A further exhibition in the Castel Sant'Angelo, Rome took place in 2009 (Volpe 2009).

Yet there has been disquiet among senior figures in the North American museum community about the return of pieces such as the Sarpedon krater. James Cuno, at the time director of the Art Institute of Chicago, argued that "cultural property is a modern political construct" at a debate in New York in March 2006, weeks after the MMA had agreed to hand the krater back to Italy. He specifically addressed the issue of the krater:

> Italy is making claims on objects that are, in the case of the Euphronios krater, 2,500 years old. The state itself is only 170 years old.

In his view the fact that the krater was placed in an Etruscan tomb (if that is where it was deposited) more than two thousand years before the creation of the modern state of Italy, this was part of world, or cosmopolitan, culture and thus should be displayed in a "world-class" museum such as the Metropolitan Museum. Cuno seemed to suggest that Italy had no rights of ownership. This of course overlooks the contemporary legal protection of Italian archaeological sites and the movement of archaeological objects from Italy itself. Cuno did not address the more important issue that the modern Italian state is the rightful steward of these world heritage sites and objects.

Cuno himself is probably sensitive about archaeological material from Italy as in 1995 he was director of Harvard's art museums when they acquired 182 fragments of Attic pottery (Gill 2010a:5–6). The fragments were purchased from a New York dealer who had acquired them from Robert Guy. He in turn was said to have acquired the pieces from friends and dealers. Certainly there was no documentary evidence that the pieces were known prior to 1971 (Watson and Todeschini 2006:235–236).

The curatorial staff at the MMA also seem unconcerned about the return of antiquities from the Department of Greek and Roman Art to both Italy and Turkey. Carlos Picón (in Picón et al. 2007:19), the present curator, in commenting on the Sarpedon krater, the Lydian silver hoard, and the "Morgantina" hoard observed:

> The last quarter-century or so has witnessed a dramatic change in the climate for acquiring all kinds of antiquities, not just classical. Yet real appreciation of and interest in ancient art have hardly diminished, and the legal ramifications of collecting in these fields remain to be charted to the understanding and satisfaction of both the private sector and the public domain.

In a separate interview for the *New Yorker*, Picón passed the comment, "Treasure hunting used to be thought of as something very worthy ... Now someone goes into his back yard and excavates a coin and it is called 'looting' and 'rape,' and all this" (Mead 2007:55). Such militant views have not gone unnoticed and brought a strong rebuke: "this very storm over Dr. Picón's comments may have served to stress to the Metropolitan Trustees, its director, and all its curators, that the time of illicit acquisitions (whether by gift, loan, or purchase) is long gone" (Ridgway 2007).

North American scholars are sensing that attitudes need to change. Stephen L. Dyson (2007) in his review of *The Medici Conspiracy* noted that some in the museum world have yet to recognize the problems. No doubt he was thinking of the public debate held immediately after the return of the Sarpedon krater had been announced:

> a counter-offensive is already under way in centres of museum power, especially in the United States. It is being led by powerful and largely unrepentant museums, supported by compliant journalists and academics, and ultimately financed by wealthy collectors who want to see themselves once again depicted as modern-day Maecenases and not as contemporary robber barons. Their justifications rest on the latest version of cultural imperialism, now bearing labels like 'cosmopolitanism' by which the dominant political, military and economic power claims that it embodies civilization and asserts the right to gather unto itself the looted treasures of the world.

Although one of these "modern-day Maecenases" had to return part of her collection to Italy in 2008, it is likely that the campaign by senior museum figures to continue to acquire recently surfaced antiquities will continue (see Cuno 2008).

Conclusion

The life-cycle of the Sarpedon krater started in one of the potters' quarters of the city of Athens at the end of the archaic period. It perhaps then was shipped to Etruria in Italy where it was (probably) used as one of the objects placed in a monumental tomb (perhaps in Cerveteri). Sometime in the early 1970s (possibly late 1971) *tombaroli* opened the Etruscan tomb and removed their pieces. The krater then travelled through the network of middlemen and agents until it came into the possession of Robert Hecht. It was offered to the MMA and after much negotiation the money was paid. But its travels were not over: in 2008 the krater returned to Italy as a reminder of lost archaeological contexts and as a warning for museums not to acquire recently surfaced antiquities.

4

Moot Loot Speaks: Classical Archaeology and the Displaced Object

STEPHEN L. DYSON

The classical archaeologist, more than any other archaeologist, works with objects without context. Since the rise of the Roman Empire and especially since the Renaissance, tens of thousands of objects, ranging from massive statues to small bronzes, have been ripped from their archaeological contexts and dispatched far from their places of origins, initial use, and final deposition. Most points of standard archaeological reference, both locational and chronological, have been lost. The temporal placement, cultural significance, and even the authenticity must be reconstructed by other means. It is not accidental that the classical archaeologists in the nineteenth century, heirs to this chaos, became pioneers in typological analysis and masters in the construction of stylistically-based chronological sequences. It was the only way to make order out of the uprooted.

However, while the objects—mainly statues, vases, and other pieces of "high art"—were losing much of their basic archaeological context, they were acquiring others. Those new meanings were cultural and ideological, expressions of their roles as icons of cosmopolitan civilization and especially its Western manifestations in the classical tradition. That reembodiment often had little to do with their original place within Greek or Roman cultural, social, and economic systems. However, in a postprocessual rather than a processual world of archaeological interpretation, the accumulation of this latter patina has its own interests and its own current relevance. Indeed, the market demands created by those cultural and ideological constructs that in turn has developed around devotion to the

43

classical tradition drives the looting and site destruction that goes on today. It threatens the integrity of large sectors of the archaeological record. The relationship between ideological constructs and physical displacement within classical archaeology will be the central focus of this essay.

The Classical Background

This impulse to loot artistic treasures for their artistic worth and their symbolic associations began early in Greco-Roman history. So did the ideal of later, more benevolent conquerors returning treasures to their original contexts. The Persians, as part of their sack of Athens in 480 B.C., carried off certain works of art to their homeland. Those were returned to Athens after Alexander the Great conquered the Persian Empire (Miles 2008:24–44). The Carthaginians seized works of art during the sacking of Greek cities in Sicily. The Romans, when they conquered Carthage, returned some of those objects to their cities of origins.

However, the Romans themselves took the looting of works of art to a new height (Miles 2008). Beginning with their conquests of Italian cities in the third century B.C. and massively expanding with their conquest of the Greek cities and centers of the Eastern Mediterranean in the second century B.C., the Romans stripped temples, precincts, and civic centers of their artistic treasures and carted the loot back to Rome. In some situations this was just looting for the sake of looting. In others cases, works were taken because they were already considered artistic treasures and were executed by artists whose names were already famous in the canon of great art. Situational context was lost, but that was replaced by enhanced cultural meaning. They no longer stood in the place where they were dedicated, but they acquired new meaning by being "treasures" in the great "museum" of classical art.

It should be emphasized that one aspect of context largely remained intact even as the works of art were transported from Greece to Rome. That was the sacred. In Rome the looted objects were generally displayed in sacred space. It was part of what the Romans called *evocatio,* the formal calling of the gods from a city conquered by Rome. The Roman authorities generally frowned on the private appropriation of sacred art. Much of our knowledge about the "art business" in this era comes from the speeches that Cicero prepared against a governor of Sicily named Verres.

One of Cicero's major lines of attack centered on Verres's "privatization" of sacred art (Miles 2008:105–151).

The presence of so much great Greek art stimulated cultural taste among the Roman elite and also a desire to possess. They wanted to decorate with art their great urban residences, their country villas, and the more secular public buildings that they commissioned. They wanted not only "museum-quality" pieces, but also thematic displays that ranged from representations of learned philosophers to notorious prostitutes. To meet that demand, methods and mechanical copying were developed. Greek artists, capable of creating "originals" that embodied and reworked classical styles, were imported to Rome. Thousands of Roman copies of Greek originals flooded the market. The National Museum at the Palazzo Massimo in Rome displays three, almost totally similar copies of the *Discus Thrower* created by the fifth century B.C. Greek sculptor Myron. They were presumably created in Rome. By their placement in ancient public and private settings they acquired a new set of contexts related to both creation and consumption.

This massive looting of art should have left the great sanctuaries of Greece threadbare, but the A.D. second-century traveler Pausanias has much to say about the works of art that were still to be found in civic and sacred spaces during his day. Some insight into the reality of the situation may be provided by the discovery of the statue designated the *Hermes of Praxiteles* by German archaeologists at Olympia in the late-nineteenth century. Pausanias had described a statue of Hermes in the exact place where the archaeologists found it nearly seventeen centuries later. What better proof of the fact that we were dealing with an original work of Greek art and its original context? Many archaeologists still accept those premises, but others raise serious doubts. The Hermes, which is still to be seen in the Olympia Museum, has support struts and other technical indicators that suggest that it is a marble copy of a bronze original. It may have been a late replacement (De Grummond 1996:588).

The emperor Nero was notorious for carrying off Greek statues even from sanctuaries. He visited Olympia, where he participated in the Olympic Games. It is hard to believe that he resisted this refined statue carved by one of Greece's greatest sculptors, a work that would have appealed to the taste of Rome's greatest imperial aesthete. It seems very likely that the original Hermes was at that time ripped from its original context and carted to Rome. Like so many original Greek works of art, it probably perished in one of Rome's many fires or was turned into lime in the Middle Ages. The Olympians lost not only a sacred object, but also a tourist attraction. The easiest solution was to resort to the Roman practice of statue copying, place the reproduction in the original location, and keep silent about the background to this new-looking work of art. They fooled Pausanias and many classical archaeologists.

Copying and collecting classical art continued down to the end of Roman power. Some of our best collections of ancient sculpture were found in late villas in remote locations in Spain and France (Stirling 2005). Even the triumph of Christianity did not entirely end the practice of collecting. However, the collapse of the Roman Empire, the loss of interest in much of classical culture, and the consolidation of Christianity's power meant both a much reduced interest in pagan statuary and the destruction of many sites and much material. The ultimate loss of object and context came often when statues were fed into the lime kilns that are ubiquitous in the medieval levels of so many classical sites. However, the processes of displacement were not totally and blindly destructive. Fragments of antiquity in the form of pieces of architecture and sculpture, what medieval archaeologists called *spolia*, were displayed and reincorporated especially into churches in many parts of the former Greco-Roman world. The practice was very common in Rome. The recycled fragments represented a grudging identity with antiquity, even as they celebrated the triumph of Christianity over paganism (De Lachenal 1995).

Renaissance Background

With the Renaissance the "playing field" changed. The identification with classical antiquity became central to European culture, and massive efforts were made to recover all aspects of the lost civilizations of Greece and Rome (Weiss 1969). The ancient objects became especially valued as physical embodiments of the glories of ancient Greece and Rome. The artists sought them for models, and the humanist collectors for inspiration. Ancient sites were looted like mines, often secretly and with little appreciation for the larger archaeological picture to which the looted objects belonged. However, specific contexts were noted if they enhanced the associative value of an object. When the famous statue of Laocoon was discovered in Rome in the early sixteenth century, the association of the find spot with the ruins of the ancient Baths of Titus enhanced its importance.

The Roman writer Pliny the Elder had mentioned that a Laocoon was to be found in that location in his day. He also identified the sculptors who had actually carved it. Suddenly, Renaissance artists and humanists were placed in the presence of an ancient work of art, whose credentials were confirmed by ancient written sources (Settis 1999).

The complexity of context was increased by the growth of the culture of collecting. Kings, nobles, cardinals, and popes all sought to create collections of ancient works of art (Haskell and Penny 1981). The main emphasis was on sculpture, with palaces filling up with groups of portrait busts and Greco-Roman gods. Restorers were hired to make battered fragments look like respectable wholes, and antiquarian scholars employed to catalog and identify the works, most of whose ancient context had been lost. The mania for collecting spread throughout Europe, especially within the nobility of England. During the middle decades of the eighteenth century young English nobles arrived in Italy on what became known as the Grand Tour (Hibbert 1987). The tour saw much debauchery, but also the growth of a serious interest in the collecting of works of antiquity. Large numbers of ancient works were shipped north of the Alps, forming the bases of extensive collections in stately homes, some of which still survive today.

This long period of collecting created another type of context that is distinctive for classical archaeology: that is the context of the collection history of individual pieces. A sculpture that was unearthed by a sixteenth-century humanist, donated to a Roman cardinal, sold to a British nobleman, who in turn sold it to an American robber baron, who in turn donated it to a major Boston or New York museum, has acquired associations that are as much part of the context history as the original location in the peristyle of the Latin villa from whose ruins it had been looted. Not surprisingly, the study of the history of collecting with all of its cultural associations has become one of the most dynamic subfields of classical archaeology.

The history of classical archaeology up to the early nineteenth century had been largely a "Roman" history. Most of the works collected had been Roman creations. They were found in Roman contexts and had been collected by modern Romans. Scholars were certainly aware that there was a Greek cultural context behind this Roman cultural world, but that remained secondary to their antiquarian and aesthetic agendas. Three events in the later eighteenth and early nineteenth centuries changed that.

Nationalism and Archaeological Provenience

The first event was the publication in 1764 of a new history of ancient art written by German savant Johannes Winckelmann (Winckelmann 2006). Operating within the context of his great antiquarian learning, Winckelmann provided an evolutionary reconstruction of ancient art, which placed its high point in the Greek world of the fifth century B.C., and relegated the art of Rome to the realms of decadence and decline. Winckelmann worked, of course, with the same written classical sources that had been used since the Renaissance and developed his ideas on the primacy of Greek art through the intense study of Roman copies and creations in the collections of Rome. He saw almost no original Greek art. However, he created a new value scheme that placed the Hellenic at the center of the study of ancient art (Potts 1994).

The second event was the arrival in London of the marbles that Lord Elgin had removed from the Parthenon in Athens. Elgin was a collector in the Grand Tour tradition, but on a scale that surpassed efforts of the drunken young lords. He was also influenced by the growing interest in classical Greek architecture in cultivated British circles. His position as a British ambassador to the Ottoman sultan gave him special powers and influence. The small Byzantine city of Athens, not the international center of Rome, became the object of his depredations, as he removed crate after crate of Acropolis marbles and dispatched them to London.

Almost immediately, Elgin became a focus of controversy, more in London than in sleepy, disinterested Athens (Hitchens 1987; St. Clair 1998). He was immediately criticized by some for his removal of so much Greek art from its original context. Certain connoisseurs, whose view of classical art was shaped by the world of restored copies that had dominated classical archaeology since the fifteenth century, did not take immediately to the battered originals. That problem was exacerbated by Elgin's then-unprecedented decision to not have the marbles restored. Finally, the Parthenon sculptures were accepted by the British state and became the centerpieces of the collection of the British Museum. If Elgin had little respect for context, he did help promote the cult of the original. Roman copies and plaster casts gradually ceased to be central to the world of collectors and museums. Both private collectors and museum curators wanted originals, and they wanted Greek originals. That quest, which accelerated during the nineteenth century, promoted in its turn massive site and context destruction.

The third element in the shift toward Hellenism was the rise of Greek nationalism and the use of the classical past to advance the goals of that nationalism. When the Hellenic national movement began in the late-eighteenth and early-nineteenth centuries, Greece was a small Christian province of the Ottoman Empire (Dyson 2006:72–79). Its historical identity was more with the Byzantine Empire that had been destroyed in the mid-fifteenth century and not with the remote, pagan past. It was Greek intellectuals, many of them living in exile outside of their homeland, who turned to their classical and, especially, their Attic past to create a "dream nation" that found its roots in the distant world of Hellenic glory (Hamilakis and Yalouri 1999). The making of Athens into the capital and symbolic center of the new nation meant making the classical visible and the postclassical invisible. Strict laws were passed that gave the Greeks total control over the access to their archaeological past. At the same time, the Greeks themselves could be ruthless at highlighting and obliterating approved and nonapproved archaeological expressions of that past.

No site expressed that better than the Acropolis, which became a central symbol for the Greek nation (Yalouri 2001). The drumbeat of demand for the recovery of the Elgin marbles began then, and it continues up to the present. At the same time the complex post-Periclean physical history of the rock through its Roman Byzantine and Ottoman history was swept away with little respect for the information it might provide on the changing uses of the Acropolis. The Acropolis became a tabula rasa on which both the Hellenes and Hellene-inspired Westerners could create their own "dream history" of the Periclean Golden Age.

Archaeology and the ideological formation of the Italian nation were more complex, for successful nationalism came to Italy later and had more diverse, European roots. Rome with its long papal history posed problems for a secular nation that was, in many respects, created in opposition to the Roman Catholic Church. In the end, the impulse toward *Roma Capitale* prevailed, and in September of 1870 Italian forces seized Rome.

The new capital was a sleepy papal city, where the ruins played a secondary role to the hundreds of churches and other religious monuments. The new capital rapidly expanded in the decades after 1870 with much destruction of the archaeological record and to the benefit of the antiquities trade (Bolton 1970:38–162; Hibbert 1985:244–285). However, the new secular government also turned to the ancient Roman monuments and to the archaeologists to provide an alternative vision of the urban past, one linked to the glories of ancient Rome (Barbanera 1998:34–48). Pioneering efforts were made to create an extensive archaeological zone in the center of the city that was focused on the ancient Roman Forum, which was still largely unexcavated. The initial excavation program centered, like that of the Acropolis, on clearing most of the forum down to the "glory periods" of ancient Rome. For nineteenth-century Italians that was the Later Republic and the Early Empire. Little attention was paid to the complexity of the archaeological record, until at the turn of the century the excavations undertaken by Giacomo Boni turned to the illumination of the earliest century of occupation in the Roman Forum (Barbanera 1998:82–86).

During this same time period a new, more systematic archaeological discipline was being created, especially in the German universities and museums (Marchand 1996). Central to this new archaeology was the creation of evolutionary histories of the development of major categories of artistic forms, especially for sculpture and for later vases. Scholars such as the great German archaeologist Adolph Furtwangler combined ancient literary references and surviving marbles to write a history of Greek sculpture that combined long-term stylistic evolution with the reconstructions of the creations of great Greek artists (De Grummond 1996:475–476). It was largely an artificial schema, but one that had scholarly legitimacy. Classical archaeologists now had a new art historical reconstruction of Greek sculpture. It also provided a framework into which could be fitted the so-called Roman copies of Greek originals, sculptures found in new excavations in Greece and the Eastern Mediterranean, and the growing body of undocumented material that increasingly flooded the antiquities market.

The great body of ancient material that had lost its original site context was now placed in this new created context, which provided the archaeological connoisseur with much-needed information about origins, stylistic identity, and possibly even the artist who had created the original, if not the ancient copy possessed by the collector. Moreover, this world of context was not one of dirt and obscure stratigraphy, the domain of antiquarians or hardly-more-appealing scientific archaeologists. It was one linked to the discourse of high culture, of universal beauty, and the transcendent message of the classical idea. Twentieth-century classical collections, built largely around Greek sculpture and Greek vases, have developed around the artificial context-creating activities of sculptural experts like the classical curator at the Metropolitan Museum of Art Gisela Richter and the vase connoisseur John Beazley (Dyson 1998:122–157, 2006:133–171). They have been fortified by the rhetoric of eternal classicism.

However, nationalistic agendas based on archaeology did not die, and the twentieth century saw numerous examples of the creation of new, self-serving ideological contexts for particular archaeological environments. Most striking were the activities of the Fascists in Italy (Manacorda and Tamassia 1985). During their long period of power (1922–1943) they sought systematically to reposition surviving Roman remains to serve less to illuminate ancient Rome and more to relate the "old" Rome of Caesar and Augustus to the "new" Rome of Benito Mussolini. Ironically, in an age when archaeologists like Mortimer Wheeler were highlighting the important of contextual and especially stratigraphic control, Mussolini's archaeologists devastated archaeological setting to emphasize ideological setting. The most blatant example was the parade route that Mussolini built from the Colosseum to the Palazzo Venezia, where he had his official residence. It cut through the sites of the fora built by some of the greatest of Roman emperors. Parts of the complexes were buried under the parade route. Others sections were ruthlessly cleared and rapidly restored to serve as "stage" settings for the Fascist displays. True archaeological context was destroyed, and a new ideological context created. That Fascist ideological context was to influence more purely archaeological agendas at those and other archaeological sites in Rome in eras well after the fall of Fascism.

Rise of the Antiquities Market

The post–World War II era has largely seen the end of the more blatant archaeological atrocities in classical lands. Indeed, the 1950s and the 1960s represented a golden age of scientific excavations in the Mediterranean, projects that equaled in quality the best mega-digs in the New World. Projects in Greece, Italy, and Turkey enriched classical archaeology and provided models for the rest of the archaeological profession. Stratigraphic excavation, careful recording, and full publication have created a world of context-rich objects. The type site for this modern classical archaeology remains the Athenian Agora (Camp 1986).

The activity in archaeology was part of a wider revival of interest in the classics in post–World War II America. That new "classicism" was especially embraced by the cultural elite, who benefited economically from the "boom years." That elite bankrolled the excavations, because they wanted to expand our knowledge about that classical past. They also created their own private collections, so that they, like Renaissance nobles and eighteenth-century English lords, could possess a piece of that precious past. Their patronage extended over into the public sphere of the art museums. New museums like the Getty were founded on the basis of massive private collections. In other instances they provided the objects or the financial resources that allowed established museums to expand their holdings in ancient art (Meyer 1973).

A supply system had to be in place to meet the demand for Greek and Roman works of art. By the end of the nineteenth century, an international network of traders in antiquities had been created. Since countries such as Greece, Italy, and Turkey established ever-more rigorous laws on the looting of archaeological sites and the export of antiquities, such a market had to operate at the margins of visibility and legality (Watson and Todeschini 2006; Waxman 2008). Some of the material came from old collections that were broken up and sold on the markets. Most came from the looting of archaeological sites. A certain amount came from the workshops of ingenious forgers (Sox 1987).

Under such circumstances, questions of context became more complicated. The buyer wanted to know enough about origins to determine that the work of art was not a fake. The scientist and the connoisseur were supposed to provide that information. On the other hand, the buyer did not want too much detailed context information. It might become clear that the object had been looted and exported from a specific archaeological site in violation of some national law. The "safest" context was that which was established by placing the object in the evolutionary history of classical art that had been developed by the classical archaeologists of the later-nineteenth and early-twentieth century. Grubby archaeological information would be replaced by high culture meaning.

That mode of collection culminated in the early 1970s with the acquisition by the Metropolitan Museum of Art of the so-called million dollar Greek pot (Hoving 1993:307–340). Vase connoisseurs, using systems of dating and artist identity developed by experts like John Beazley, assigned the pot to Athens of the early fifth century B.C., a fine product by an artisan named Euphronios. Almost immediately rumors circulated that the vase had been looted from an Etruscan tomb and had made its way to New York through the complex, clandestine networks of the antiquities market. Few in the museum world cared about the loss of archaeological information that had attended the acquisition of the pot. For them the context was not that of a Greek trade object found in Italy, but an expression of universal Hellenic beauty made at the high point of the Greek golden age.

Conclusions

The classical archaeological community finally reacted to what was becoming an epidemic of site destruction throughout the Mediterranean. The lines of battle were laid down for a conflict that continues up to the present day. Professional associations like the Archaeological Institute of America took steps to ensure that they did not become unwitting accomplices in the legitimatization of looted objects. Archaeological administrators in the countries most affected by the looting, such as Italy and Turkey, benefited from the increasingly public debate about the antiquities trade to take increasingly strong administrative steps. Those steps ranged from international law suits and threats to withholding excavation permits to even the trial of prominent antiquities dealers and museum curators. Threats of expensive litigation or even of time spent in a Mediterranean jail helped make a significant dent in the international market.

However, the forces promoting the importance of higher cultural meaning have counterattacked against those defending more traditional archaeological context. They claim a "high ground" on the issue of who should control not only the ideological but also the physical possession of the past. The leading defenders of the right of possession are generally figures from the museum world with high-level administrators like James Cuno of the Art Institute of Chicago leading the charge (Cuno 2008, 2009). At the base level of arguments, many of the national claims have been dismissed as the sour pleas of countries like Italy that cannot effectively protect their own archaeological heritage. However, the museum phalanx has also attempted to raise the level of discourse, returning to the rhetoric of "elevated" classicism, as it developed in the nineteenth and twentieth centuries. Drawing heavily on the ideas of Princeton University philosophy professor Kwame Appiah (Appiah 2006), they defend their collecting practices as promoting a "truth and beauty" cosmopolitanism. A vase or statue that can be contextualized within such exalted parameters does not need the narrow stratigraphic associations of the grubby world of modern scientific archaeology.

The sad reality is that most of the time classical archaeologists will continue to live in a world where most of the objects they study are largely without what has become regarded today as established, quality disciplinary context. That does not mean that we should abandon efforts to save what is left of the archaeological record or to combat "cultural myths" that promote its destruction. However, a discipline like classical archaeology, with its long and rich history, has much to teach about creating orders and contexts of other sorts and significances for objects from the past that are orphans in the archaeological record.

5

Unprovenienced Artifacts and the Invention of Minoan and Mycenaean Religion

SENTA C. GERMAN

In February 2009 the Brooklyn Museum of Art opened an exhibition entitled "Coptic Sculpture in the Brooklyn Museum," the focus of which was to reveal the fact that one-third of the museum's collection of these objects is fake (Russmann 2009). Mostly collected in the 1960s and 1970s, the sculptures can be traced back to major antiquities dealers in New York and Switzerland and then ultimately to Egypt where they were produced. Scholars of Coptic art have been aware of the fakes for years (Spanel 2001; Vikan 1981), yet the museum kept the pieces on view, maintaining their authenticity. Brooklyn's collection of Coptic sculpture is the second largest in North America and not the only one amassed from questionable sources. The Princeton University Art Museum, the Hirshhorn Museum in Washington, D.C., the Staatliche Museen in Berlin, and the Icon Museum in Recklinghuasen all acquired many pieces at the same time, and many believe there are a number of fakes in those collections as well. The Coptic pieces that emerged around the 1960s and 1970s were originally hailed as representing one of the largest groups of sculptures to have survived anywhere from the early Christian era, functioning as an artistic bridge between pagan and Christian cultures and evidence of the continuity of large-scale figural sculpture from the classical period. We now know most of the pieces are fake, and a robust continuity of sculptural forms between the fifth and mid-seventh centuries in Egypt must be reexamined. Without this extraordinary and frank exhibit at the Brooklyn Museum, such a reexamination would likely not take place, and certainly the lay public would know nothing of the fakes. The following essay is about similar misrepresentations, especially to the lay public, ultimately based on fake and unprovenienced materials, those which are used in reconstructions of Minoan and Mycenaean religion.

* * *

As with nearly all things related to the Aegean Bronze Age, the study of the religion practiced during this era begins with Sir Arthur J. Evans. Four years before Evans broke ground at Knossos on Crete in 1900, he delivered a paper at the anthropological section of the British Association at Liverpool entitled "Tree and Pillar Worship in Mycenaean Greece" that was the first attempt at the topic (Evans 1896).[1] Indeed, Evans's interest in Minoan religion was a life-long passion and very much influenced by the mythological and cult research of the late-nineteenth and early-twentieth centuries. Specifically, Evans was influenced by the work of Johann Jakob Bachofen (1861), among others, who argued for a matriarchal stage of development in all early societies. Moreover, Evans insisted that the roots of later classical Greek culture were in the Bronze Age remains of Crete and, therefore, was eager to find the first glimpses of Iron Age cult in the remains he uncovered at Knossos. That Evans brought many preconceptions to his work at Knossos has been well established (see, for example, MacEnroe 1995; MacGillivray 2000). What has not been discussed is how the religious and mythological framework of the Aegean Bronze Age that he developed was based on, in considerable measure, unprovenienced, faked, or incorrectly reconstructed artifacts.

The Beginning of the Problem

In Evans's first substantial work on Minoan religion (Evans 1901) he identified what would become the core concepts in its study: the practice of worship of the sacred tree and pillar, the cult equipment of the double axe and "horns of consecration," as well as the predominance of female deities. The method Evans employed in this study was comparative, setting the Bronze Age data next to other antique (and largely pre-classical) evidence and rendering "logical" interpretations, essentially like a syllogism. The "data" or raw materials on which he based his work were largely from his own excavations at Knossos: wall paintings, pottery, architectural remains, and small finds.

Sadly, with regard to both Evans's method and data, the seeds of a now century-long problem were sewn. As for method, Evans's comparative materials came from grossly distant lands and eras, ranging from the Northern European Neolithic to Bronze Age India to Iron Age Normandy. Thus, the comparative study of various strands of evidence was made (many of which have been since discounted as illegitimate comparanda, including undatable mythology and ethnohistory) of totally unrelated areas. And, as for the data, there was another significant fault. Alongside legitimately excavated pieces Evans included several others of highly dubious origins, either bought on the art market or "acquired" by travelers on Crete. The numbers are not insignificant. Specifically, of 53 objects discussed in the article, 11, or 21 percent, have no archaeological provenience whatsoever.[2] Most of the objects are stamp seals that illustrate cultic furniture and ceremonies, lending evidence in Evans's argument for their important role in Minoan religion. The problem with using unprovenienced objects is that theories based on them, at best, must be regarded suspiciously and, at worst, are false.

The Palace of Minos (Evans 1921, 1928, 1930, 1935), the five-volume publication of Evans's excavations, contains several passages that are exclusively concerned with reconstructing cult spaces, objects, and religious practice. When reviewing these passages it is striking how many feature either heavily reconstructed objects or have no archaeological provenience. Moreover, many of the objects in his discussions are some of the best known of the era. For instance, the first volume introduces none other than the Snake Goddess, undeniably the most famous object to emerge from the excavations and one of the most commonly reproduced pieces of ancient art (Evans 1921:495–523). The Snake Goddess, however, is in large measure restored. The remains of the statuette were found incomplete (lacking the head and right arm), together with pieces of two other similar figurines distributed between two stone-lined pits called the Temple Repositories. How the figurine was reconstructed and, more importantly, with which pieces, is obscure because the excavation notes and their publication do not include the exact findspots of the materials in the Repositories (Lapatin 2002:60–64; Panagiotaki 1993:84–86). Moreover, there are no surviving notes that reveal the guiding principles of the restoration process.

Despite this, Evans reconstructs a cult of the Snake Goddess, complete with shrine. As comparanda, he uses figurines in Berlin and Boston that lack provenience, both of which have since been determined to be fakes. This model of establishing theories of Minoan cult based on questionable pieces, supported by other questionable pieces, is unfortunately not uncommon in Evans's work. For instance, in the second volume of *The Palace of Minos*, in his discussion of the Harbor Town of Knossos and the maritime trade at the site, Evans (1928:229) argues that there was a Minoan patron goddess of the harbor. As evidence he points the reader to a sculpture made of stone acquired from a dealer by the Fitzwilliam Museum since shown to be a forgery (Butcher and Gill 1993). In the same volume, Evans presents a dramatic reconstruction of a large stucco fresco depicting a striding male youth with his hand to his chest, wearing an elaborate feather crown (Evans 1928:775–795). This character Evans named the Priest King, a visual record of the theocratic rule he imagined for the Minoans. Research on the fresco fragments themselves, as well as careful study of newly discovered excavation notes, revealed in the 1980s that Evans's reconstruction contains fragments from several frescoed figures, and the crown most likely was worn by a female sphinxlike creature (Coloumb 1979, 1990; Niemeier 1987, 1988).

The third volume of *The Palace of Minos* contains several chapters that discuss religion, including chapter 74, which presents visual evidence of a Minoan "after-world." This Evans (1930:134–157) saw not unlike Hades described by Homer, and based this conclusion on his reading of the Ring of Nestor, which he had separately published in 1925, along with a group of gold rings and stamp seals known as the Thisbe Treasure. Evans purchased the Ring of Nestor in the early 1920s from a "trustworthy source" who assured him it had been found several years before in a beehive tomb at "Nestor's Pylos" by a local man. This ring is now generally regarded as a fake (Dayet 1948; Sakellarakis 1973, 1994), although there remains some dissent (Pini 1998). One scholar has reported that one of Evans's chief restorers claimed in the 1930s to have made it himself (Warren 1987:498).

Another important component of Evans's Minoan pantheon discussed in the same volume, the Boy-God, has run afoul. Specifically, in chapter 87, Evans (1930) discusses the now-acknowledged fake (Lapatin 2002) Boston Goddess and another "newly discovered" sculpture of a youthful male, which Evans called the Boy-God. His discussion of the Boy-God and his relationship to the Snake Goddess (the one legitimizing the other) revolves around fourteen objects of sculpture and seal stones. Three are known fakes (the Boston Goddess, Figure 305; the Boy-God, Evans 1930:Figure 309; and a seal from the Thisbe Treasure, Evans 1930:Figure 319); one is heavily restored (the Snake Goddess's votive, Evans 1930:Figure 306); four are totally unprovenienced (Evans 1930:Figures 308a and 308b, 320, and 322); and the remaining six are from legitimate excavations.

As Kenneth Lapatin (2002:153–175) has argued, by the late 1920s, those who were making fake Minoan objects were devoted students of Evans's model of Minoan religion and began to produce pieces that confirmed his published theories. This phenomenon is found throughout the fourth volume of *The Palace of Minos,* published in 1935. For instance, in chapter 91, Evans focuses on a "new" ivory and gold figurine, again acquired by him from a "reliable" source, which he calls "Our Lady of Sports" (Evans 1935:Figures 14 and 15), the patron goddess of bull leaping. Evans supports the authenticity of the sculpture by demonstrating its similarities to figurines that we now acknowledge as fake: the Fitzwilliam Goddess (Evans 1935:Figures 17a, 17b, 17c, 21), the Boston Goddess, (Evans 1935:Figure 20), and of course, the Snake Goddess from the Temple Repositories, genuine, but heavily restored. In chapter 95 of the same volume Evans gleans the more maternal aspects of the Snake Goddess from a "new" stone figurine of her likeness (Evans 1935:Figure 149, 150) that he reports having been found in the same deposit as the Fitzwilliam Goddess. Again, we see Evans arguing authenticity of a fake object with another fake.

The importance of *The Palace of Minos* in establishing knowledge about Aegean Bronze Age culture is difficult to exaggerate. The materials that Evans discovered at Knossos were unique and revealed an entirely new society that, prior to the turn of the century, had not been known and, more surprisingly, had been thought to be in the realm of myth. Immediately, Aegean Bronze Age material was keenly desired by museums large and small, and the Minoans and Mycenaeans were rapidly appended at the beginning of histories of classical Greece, and its religion.

In 1927, Martin Nilsson (1949) published *The Minoan-Mycenaean Religion and Its Survival in Greek Religion*. It was the first book to distinguish between Minoan and Mycenaean cult practice, by then obvious as more Mycenaean sites on the mainland had been excavated, and there was more material with which to draw a distinction. Nilsson begins with archaeological sites believed to be locations of cult, such as caves, rock shelters, and mountain peaks, and includes many recent discoveries. This analysis is followed by cult objects and images, and Nilsson makes an impressive effort to stick to those that he believes are genuine (in the introduction of the second edition [Nilsson 1949] he specifically addresses the issue of "Suspect Objects" among which he includes the Thisbe treasure, the Ring of Nestor, and several figurines). Nonetheless, there are still some problems. Of the 192 objects that Nilsson illustrates in his book, 26, or 15 percent, are either unprovenienced or thought to be fake.[3]

The use of questionable objects in the writing of pre-Greek religion continues with another prominent monograph on the topic, *The Religion of Greece in Prehistoric Times,* published in 1942 by Axel W. Persson. This book concerns itself primarily with the survival of Minoan and Mycenaean religion in classical Greek practice as well as its connections to the ancient Near East. Persson's formulations of prehistoric Greek religion focus on an outline of a vegetation cycle that he formulates from the analysis of 29 gold Minoan and Mycenaean finger rings. The assumption, first offered by Evans, was that the rings are copies of large frescos, now lost, that illustrated the mythology and religious practice of the time (Persson 1942:25–87). To date, no evidence of such a fresco cycle has been discovered. Indeed, a sizable portion of the rings that Persson uses in his analysis are problematic, either now regarded as fakes or without archaeological provenience, specifically, nine, or 31 percent, of them.[4]

Looking, then, at the first half of the twentieth century and the beginning of the study of Aegean Bronze Age religion, some generalizations can be made. First, the framework of the field was set by Evans, not only with regard to the identification of cult activities, spaces, and objects but with regard to method. Eager to narrate the images of cult he discovered, either archaeologically or otherwise, Evans composed vivid and detailed reenactments of characters and rituals with scant proof, significant portions of which are inauthentic and/or heavily reconstructed. In addition to this framework, Evans's work has the power of origins; it is the first work and sets the tone for the field. We find Evans's problematic method of the study of Aegean Bronze Age religion largely duplicated in later works on the topic.

Evolving Approaches to Minoan and Mycenaean Religion

In the second half of the twentieth century a group of works emerge on Bronze Age religion that shifted focus away from "reading" the images and toward studying the locations of ritual spaces discovered through archaeological excavation. Those studies (for instance, Gesell 1985; Renfrew 1985; Rutkowski 1986; Warren 1988), archaeologically based, gave greater importance to quantifiable data as well as more anthropologically oriented methodologies, such as ethnographic analogy and comparative religion. Moreover, given that recently excavated material constituted the essential facts of these studies, the proportion of questionable objects is very low; reconstructions are few and conservative. Conclusions from these studies include caves, with a rich array of votive objects, as very important religious locations, as are "peak sanctuaries," high-set locations that have deep layers of ash and large quantities of human and animal figurines; houses and town centers hosted cult spaces as important as those at palaces. These studies also find evidence that supports some of Evans's identifications of important cult objects, namely the double axe, altars, and sacrificial tables, and *pillar-shaped stones* or baetyls.

Alongside these archaeologically based works published at the time, there are a number of area studies that focus on the reenactment of cult, cult images, and equipment. These include, for instance, Paul Rehak (1997) on the seated goddess; "Baetylic rituals," by Peter Warren (1990); images of epiphany, by R. Hägg (1986); and Younger on bull leaping (1976, 1983, 1995). Although these studies rely on new archaeological materials, they also employ familiar objects, many of which have questionable proveniences, especially stamp seals. Common among these publications are overly zealous reconstructions, especially of cult activities. Nanno Marinatos's (1993) well-known monograph on Minoan religion is especially guilty of this (see Wright 1995).

The use of these new approaches in the study of Aegean Bronze Age religion, in combination with Evans's older, less-sound method, continues in the field today and can be seen in tandem in synthetic texts. For instance, in the recently published *Cambridge Companion to the Aegean Bronze Age* (Shelmerdine 2008), in a discussion of the iconography of Minoan gods and goddesses, the authors unproblematically compare an image from the wall paintings at the site of Akrotiri, excavated in the 1970s, with a stamp seal purchased at the antiquities bazaar at the beginning of the twentieth century (Shelmerdine 2008:169), which at least one glyptic expert believes to be fake (Betts 1965). In the same volume, in a review of protopalatial Crete, social networking analysis, a very new concept, is used to explain the koine in the material culture from the first palaces (Shelmerdine 2008:121–139). Although the continued use of problematic method is lamentable, such texts are fully annotated, and the reader is able make his or her own judgments about the evidence. In sum, the recent synthetic texts are a positive development in the study of Minoan and Myceanean religion—for all but the lay reader, who would be largely unable to distinguish between better and lesser methods employed.

Minoan and Mycenaean Religion in Teaching Texts

Indeed, those who might be least well equipped to determine the relative quality of approaches and materials used in the study of Minoan and Mycenaean religion are students. Teaching texts are not annotated but should provide reliable, synthetic, up-to-date information. The type of teaching text in which the greatest number of students are introduced to the culture of the Aegean Bronze age is an introductory humanities text. Very often, at U.S. colleges and universities, humanities classes, many of which stand at the foundation of undergraduate core curricula—tracing the history, art, literature, and religion of the West—are mandatory. The questions are, How do these texts approach the religion of the Minoans and Mycenaeans, and What sorts of materials do they use as evidence? For the purposes of this study, I have looked at the three books that, taken in combination, make up the majority share of the introductory humanities textbook market (Melanie Cutler, Pearson Education, personal communication 2009): *Discovering the Humanities* (Sayre 2009), *The Western Humanities* (Matthews and Platt 2009), and *Culture and Values: A Survey of the Humanities* (Reich and Cunningham 2009).

Four consistent problems emerge in reviewing these texts: (1) descriptions of Minoan and Mycenaean religion are generally uncritically presented, despite the fact that, unlike the religions of the Ancient Near East, Egypt, and classical Greece, the religion of the Minoans and Mycenaean has no known central religious text; (2) the majority of objects that are included in discussions of Minoan and Mycenaean religion are either fakes, heavily restored, or unprovenienced; (3) ideas about Minoan and Mycenaean religion that were developed by Evans or employ Evans's positivistic methods are repeated; and (4) there is an absence of information about Minoan and Mycenaean religion that comes from either archaeological or textual sources. Below are examples.

In Henry Sayre's *Discovering the Humanities*, chapter 5 concerns itself with the Aegean Bronze Age. Of the 11 illustrations of Minoan and Mycenaean objects sites and architecture, seven, or 66 percent, are either unprovenienced (Sayre 2009:Figure 5.2), heavily restored (Sayre 2009:Figures 5.3, 5.5, 5.9; page 139) or complete reconstructions (Sayre 2009:Figures 5.4, 5.10). Indeed, the first object illustrated is a Cycladic figurine (Sayre 2009:Figure 5.2) in the Nicholas P. Goulandris Foundation of the Dokathismata type, which has no provenience. The Goulandris collection is notorious for its unprovenienced pieces and suspected fakes, and some have argued that the collection should be regarded with great caution (Broodbank 1992). Indeed, several figurines of this same type were excavated at the end of the nineteenth century by Christos Tsountas and published in the 1970s and would have been just as instructional in illustration (for example, Doumas 1977:Figure 48).

In Sayre's discussion of Minoan goddesses, he identifies one as Britomartis, which he reports as the name of a goddess in the Minoan language, which means goddess of the mountains. This is right out of Nilsson (1949:510–512) and based on flawed, later classical Greek recollections and not from Aegean Bronze Age material. Furthermore, Linear A, the Minoan language to which Sayre must be referring, has yet to be translated, and certainly, the name Britomartis has not been identified in any texts. To his credit, Sayre (2009:139) includes a boxed call-out section in the same chapter about the Snake Goddess from Knossos, which is in essence a *précis* of the popular work of Lapatin (2002). Here, the author candidly discusses the problems with the piece, including its extensive reconstruction. Sayre (2009:Figure 5.9) is equally candid about the Mask of Agamemnon, explaining that "recent scholarship suggests that Schliemann may have added the handlebar mustache and large ears, perhaps to make the mask appear more 'heroic'" (2009:142). The scholarship to which Sayre is referring (Harrington et al. 1999) is very persuasive, and one wonders why he did not simply choose one of the other unmodified masks from the shaft graves at Mycenae with which to illustrate the glittering burial finds.

Roy Matthews and DeWitt Platt's *The Western Humanities* deals with much the same material, although fewer problematic pieces are included. Of the seven objects illustrated in the Aegean chapter, chapter 2, only three are heavily reconstructed (Matthews and Platt 2009:Figures 2.1, 2.2, and 2.3). However, in the authors' discussion of the Snake Goddess (Matthews and Platt 2009:Figure 2.2), there is no mention of the problematic nature of the piece. Later on in chapter 39, in a discussion of Mycenaean burial cult, it is stated that "near the end of their era, the

Minoans began to bury their dead in underground tombs and chambers, but neither the reason for the new burial practice nor its ritualistic meaning has been discovered." This is a reflection of Evans's century-old, Minoan-centric thinking, which denies that the island was taken over by the Mycenaeans "at the end of their era" (McDonald 1990:269–280). The burial custom to which Matthews and Platt refer is actually a Mycenaean one that was practiced by those people who at the end of the Bronze Age dominated the island.

John Reich and Lawrence Cunningham's (2009) *Culture and Values: A Survey of the Humanities* includes a discussion of the Aegean Bronze Age within the same chapter as ancient Egyptian, Ancient Near Eastern, and Prehistoric cultures. Of the 10 objects, sites, and architecture that they offer to illustrate the Minoan and Mycenaean era, six, or 60 percent, are problematic. Specifically, one piece is unprovenienced (Reich and Cunningham 2009:Figure 1.22); four are heavily restored (Reich and Cunningham 2009:Figures 1.23, 1.24, 1.28, 1.29); and one is a complete reconstruction (Reich and Cunningham 2009:Figure 1.25). The complete reconstruction is an artist's rendering of the site of Knossos in antiquity. Aside from some obvious errors in the scene (much of the west wing of the palace as well as the surrounding town are absent), it is illustrated abuzz with religious activity, including sacrificial animals and group worshipers. This brings to mind the fanciful composite reconstructions that Evans included in his original publication of *The Palace of Minos* (for instance, Evans 1935: frontispiece, plate XXXIII; Evans 1930:frontispiece, plate XXVI), which were only loosely based on archaeological finds.

Reich and Cunningham's (2009:21) discussion of the throne room at Knossos, with accompanying photograph of its heavily restored state (2009:Figure 1.23), strikes a similarly strong religious tone. In the caption to the photograph they point out the mythologically inspired griffins that flank the stone throne at the center of the north wall of the room. Unfortunately, this is one of Evans's incorrect reconstructions at the site. As was noted almost 50 years ago (Hopkins 1963), the placement of the two griffins on either side of the throne contradicts the original description of the finds in the room (Evans 1900:40), which noted griffins only painted on the Western wall and not surrounding the throne itself.

Like Matthews and Platt, Reich and Cunningham are quiet (or ignorant) about the reconstruction of the Snake Goddess (2009:23). They are, however, eager to identify her with later classical mythology, specifically the goddess Artemis. There is no evidence for this, but it is an opinion set out by Nilsson (1949:328, 510–514). Reich and Cunningham (2009:24) also do not mention the problematic nature of the Mask of Agamemnon but do point out that it is not Agamemnon himself, but rather a Mycenaean who ruled three centuries before him. This would obviously imply that the date (and actual existence!) of Agamemnon is a historical fact. In actuality, the existence of Agamemnon is not known, and the use of Homer to explicate Aegean Bronze Age materials is strongly avoided in scholarship (Bennet 1997). Unfortunately, Reich and Cunningham also say almost nothing about Mycenaean religion, despite rich sources on the topic (see below).

In this brief review of the discussion of religion found in three commonly used humanities textbooks we find an unfortunate situation. Unprovenienced objects are selected for illustrations despite the availability of essentially identical objects found from archaeological excavations. Objects that are heavily and problematically restored, and that have been shown to be such in published work, are uncritically used. Ideas about Minoan and Mycenaean religion still reflect the first wave of studies on the topic from the first half of the twentieth century: those that relied significantly on unprovenienced materials and fakes (the extent to which these misguided views about Aegean Bronze Age culture pervade the Web is remarkable and redoubles the problem within a teaching context because of students' ever-increasing reliance on online sources). The situation is especially unfortunate as reliable and fascinating information about Minoan and Mycenaean religion, drawn from primary archaeological and philological sources, is readily available. I review some of this below.

What Ought to Be in Teaching Texts

If so much of what we find about Minoan and Mycenaean religion in humanities texts is highly questionable, we might ask, what is based on good evidence and should be included instead? Of Minoan religion, in lieu of the Snake Goddess, one wonders why the Palaikastro Kouros (MacGillivray, Driessen, and Sackett 2000) is not discussed. This piece, discovered in the recent excavations of the site of Palaikastro in East Crete, is an ivory, gold, stone, and rock-crystal statue of roughly the same scale as the Snake Goddess. It is clearly of sacred value as it was found in a shrine in the center of town, originally situated on a stand, mounted on a faience disk in a position of visual prominence. This is certainly the statue of a god or important person, and discussion of such might be a welcome corrective to the belief that the most important gods in the Minoan pantheon were female.

As mentioned above, peak sanctuaries were clearly an important locus for cult on Minoan Crete. The site of Petsophas, in Eastern Crete (Rutkowski 1991) would be an excellent choice for explication as there survives significant architectural and votive remains that illustrate the importance of this type of site. In this might be discussed a special class of stone offering table that was dedicated at peak sanctuaries, some of which carry a formulaic inscription in Linear A. This inscription has been transliterated (a few words appear in both Linear A and B so the phonetic values of about 15 Linear A syllabograms can be assumed) as an offing to a single goddess, Ja-sa-sa-ra (Shelmerdine 2008:174–177).

Perhaps the most fascinating component of Minoan religion that might be included in humanities texts is human sacrifice. Two recent excavations have revealed vivid evidence for this. The first is in a building west of the palace at Knossos, in a basement room that contained cooking pots and the bones of several children. Faunal analysis indicates that the human bones had been defleshed, postmortem, using typical animal butchering techniques (Wall, Musgrave, and Warren 1986). The second example comes from the site of Anemospilia, south of Knossos, in a building that collapsed as the result of an earthquake. The excavations discovered the remains of an 18-year-old male (the skeleton so tightly contracted that he is considered to have been trussed in a fashion comparable to that of sacrificial animals illustrated in Minoan painting), lying on his right side on a platform in the center of the room. Among his bones was a bronze dagger 0.40 m long. Close beside the platform (or sacrificial altar?) stood a pillar with a trough around its base, thought to be designed to catch the blood from the sacrifice. The dead youth's bones were discolored in such a way (those on his upper left side being white, those on his lower right side being black) as to suggest the youth, estimated to have been 165 cm tall, had died from loss of blood (Sakellarakis and Sapouna-Sakellarakis 1981).

There is considerable evidence about Mycenaean religion, yet the humanities texts often do not cover the topic. Indeed, they often include a Mycenaean beehive tomb, a very impressive structure and as a burial no doubt reflective in some way of Mycenaean religious beliefs. If religion per se is discussed, often the only comment is that Mycenaean religion continues Minoan practices (for example, Matthews and Platt 2009:40). This observation is debatable, and differences in the religious practices of the two peoples are many and interesting. For instance, built places of Minoan worship are always within the plan of larger structures, such as palaces, but their Mycenaean counterparts often stand alone like temples. Also, Mycenaeans did not worship at peak sanctuaries or within caves, both of which were the most frequent locations of cult activities on Crete. In Mycenaean visual imagery there is no figure that can be convincingly connected with a Snake Goddess, nor is there any remnant of horns of consecration or double axes, both thought to be common objects of Minoan cult apparatus.

The most exciting and significant source of information about the religion of the Mycenaeans comes from the Linear B archives. The archive consists of deposits of semi-baked tablets found in the destruction levels of Mycenaean palaces reflecting the final months' administrations of these political, religious, and social centers. Although the texts are concerned exclusively with economic operations and do not include narrative of any sort such as myth, hymns, prayers, or divine law, they do enumerate offerings given to various gods and the preparations for ritual actions such as sacrifice and feasting. The names of the gods mentioned are particularly significant. For instance, at Mycenaean Knossos, divinities are mentioned in contexts dealing with offerings made to them in certain months. The methods and scheduling of sacrifices appear to be rigidly codified. The divinities mentioned are, among others: Atana (Athena), Ares, Poseidon, Zeus, Hera, Artemis, Hermes, and Dionysus.

Looking at specific tablets (humanities textbooks pride themselves in using primary sources!) on tablet Tn 316 from the palace at Pylos, gold vessels, men, and women are offered to a long list of divinities. This type of offering may indicate that these people are dedicated in service of the gods or perhaps is more evidence, this time from the Mycenaean world, of human sacrifice (Shelmerdine 2008:343). On a series of tablets also from Pylos, offerings of specially perfumed oil are made to Poseidon, the Wanasoi, the Mater Theia, the Dipsioi, and simply, to "the gods." Some of this oil is described as being specifically for "anointing," perhaps of statues or textiles belonging to deities (Killen 2001).

Lastly, a particularly evocative area of study among Mycenologists that would be a good addition to these sorts of general texts is that of feasting. Over the last 15 years, several aspects of this collective activity have been studied through a variety of archaeological remains. The well-published and authentic remains for feasting include descriptions of the special furniture used, what was served, the relationship of this activity to sacrifice as well as fragmentary wall paintings that illustrate group meals (Wright 2004).

Conclusions

The extent to which our understanding of the Minoan and Mycenaean religion was invented without regard for authentic data is, of course, debatable, and this is the concern of scholars in the field. The debate is a part of the messy process of scholarship, lurching and weaving its way toward evermore widely accepted narratives. What ends up in teaching texts should be based on authentic sources and reflect the most recent and established methods and knowledge. Certainly, scholars of the Aegean Bronze Age should care about what is in teaching texts, not least because if through them an interest in their field is sparked, this can translate into a host of beneficial outcomes (increased enrollments in Aegean courses and increased popularity of the field, both of which translate to more jobs and more funding for research). Yet, through the persistent use of poor methodology, which allows for the continued celebration of false and fake pieces, the field is misrepresented and our knowledge tainted. The provocative show about Coptic forgeries at the Brooklyn Museum might serve as a direction forward. Let the frank discussion of what is fake and overly reconstructed and restored begin, so we can let fall away old arguments based on these and build more authentic knowledge about Minoan and Mycenaean culture.

Notes

1. This was when all Bronze Age Greek materials were called *Mycenaean*.
2. The objects with no provenience are found illustrated Figures 9, 10, 31, 34, 39, 40, 43, 44, 45, 56, and 59.
3. The objects with no provenience are found illustrated in Nilsson 1949:Figures 7, 15, 16, 52, 56, 65, 74, 75, 76, 90, 112, 113, 128, 129, 130, 131, 132, 140, 141, 150, 155, 185, 186, 187, 190, and 204.
4. Ring numbers 1, 6, 7, 12, 17, 19, 20, 26, and 29 (Persson 1942).

6

Early Looting and Destruction of Australian Shipwreck Sites: Legislation, Education, and an Amnesty for Long-Term Preservation

JENNIFER RODRIGUES

Over 7,000 known vessels have been wrecked off the coast of Australia since the seventeenth century, leaving valuable archaeological evidence about trade, technology, social and political status, life on board, European colonization, and survival. As time went by and diving technology improved, more people were able to venture underwater to appreciate the natural undersea environment, but this also resulted in the discovery of shipwrecks, sometimes accidentally and sometimes intentionally. In Australia, the early shipwreck discoveries from the 1950s sparked an intense period of activity by recreational divers and scrap-metal collectors that included blowing up shipwrecks or collecting old relics for souvenirs. As well, there were those in Western Australia with the foresight to try to protect those wrecks for their archaeological value and for future generations to be able to appreciate.

The commonwealth government of Australia enacted the Historic Shipwrecks Act in 1976 in response to the destruction being caused to Western Australia's Dutch East India Company shipwrecks, dating back to 1629, as well as to honor its obligations under the 1972 Australian and Netherlands Committee Concerning Old Dutch Shipwrecks (ANCODS) agreement.[1] This essay is an assessment of Australia's approach in dealing with such activities and the effectiveness of its methods in regulating the privately held collections of shipwreck objects that resulted from these activities across the country. It also highlights certain issues that have been observed over the 30 intervening years that need to be dealt with in a specific and sensitive manner.

Some significant early events are highlighted, particularly in Western Australia, that caused the disturbance and destruction of the oldest known wrecks. In addition, evidence observed on site and reports by divers in subsequent years concerning souvenir hunting of other wreck sites in both remote and metropolitan regions also emerged and are briefly described. Most of the earlier problems with shipwreck disturbances across the country were dealt with by archaeological excavations and the establishment of maritime archaeology programs, which spread throughout the country. However, the problem of existing private collections still lingered in the background.

Following the enactment of blanket protection on April 1, 1993 (whereby all wrecks that turn 75 years old since wrecking are automatically protected under the Historic Shipwrecks Act 1976) and via a nationwide amnesty declared a month later, Australia attempted to recover as much information as possible from privately held collections. The primary aim was to enhance information about its maritime heritage, expand awareness about protective shipwreck legislation and custodians' obligations under the act, regulate the movement of private shipwreck relics between collectors, as well as ensure that divers were not unfairly placed in legal jeopardy due to the enactment of blanket protection.

Significant Early Events

Protective shipwreck legislation relating to commonwealth waters in Australia, which came into effect on December 15, 1976 (Jeffrey 1997:45), was introduced in response to wrecks being blown up, destroyed in other ways (e.g., tools and dredging), and souvenir-hunted by recreational divers and fishermen either opportunistically or intentionally. Moves to protect shipwrecks began first in Western Australia where the oldest known wrecks are found and where some of the oldest carried valuable coins, bullion, and rare cargo items. Unfortunately, the 1960s represented a painful beginning for Western Australia in terms of the state government's efforts to curtail the ongoing destruction of shipwrecks and to try to legally protect the sites. The State Museum tried to assemble legislation, infrastructure, and expertise to halt the remarkable destruction being caused mainly by one person using gelignite, but also by other sou-

Figure 1. Diver holding an astrolabe at the *Vergulde Draeck* site (Photo: WA Museum).

venir hunters, casual divers, and scrap-metal collectors (Henderson 1990:19; Hosty and Stuart 1994:9).

In the 1960s, there were regular reports coming from fishermen and skin divers in Western Australia about explosions that reverberated around the waters south of Ledge Point on the mid-west coast (Henderson 1993:60; Kennedy 1998:31). These were caused by blasting of the second-oldest known Dutch VOC shipwreck, the *Vergulde Draeck* (*Gilt Dragon*), which sank in 1656 (see Figure 1). The site was first discovered in 1963 by a group of Perth skin divers who were spearfishing in the area (Flowers 2001:1; Green 1985:8–9). Shortly after the 1963 discovery, the site was blasted, allegedly by someone from the same group. The first visible change observed was the absence of fish and reduction in the variety of busy underwater life. Fragmented elephant tusks, broken ballast bricks, scraps of ancient timber, pottery sherds all lay in "jumbled confusion" (Henderson 1993:60). Around June and July 1970 archaeologists also uncovered evidence of blasting and the crude use of crowbars at the *Batavia* (1629) wreck site (Henderson 1993:117) after local divers discovered it in 1963 (although fishermen in the area claimed to have discovered it earlier but had not reported it) (Cramer 1999:80). The *Batavia* came to grief near Beacon Island in the Houtman Abrolhos, also off the mid-west coast, after it hit Morning Reef. Local divers have observed that the *Batavia* had been souvenir-hunted on several occasions (Cramer 1999:316) presumably by fishermen based seasonally in the Abrolhos as well as souvenir hunters and recreational divers. The *Batavia* is the oldest of the four Dutch shipwrecks and the second-oldest known shipwreck in Western Australia. It also has a fascinating history involving a mutiny and the massacre of 125 men, women, and children, and this has been known to attract divers to the site who are intrigued by the historical events that unfolded after the vessel collided with Morning Reef.

One of the saddest events in Western Australia was the deliberate and planned destruction of Australia's earliest known shipwreck, the *Trial* (*Tryall*), with the use of gelignite. Following a very long and meticulous process of research by a few enthusiastic individuals, the *Trial*, which sank off the Monte Bello Islands near the northwest coast of Australia in 1622 (see Figure 2), was finally discovered in May 1969. The finders observed that the site appeared to consist of a fair-sized vessel with about 20 cannons surprisingly well preserved (Henderson 1993:88). However, shortly after the discoverers left the scene, the site was blasted apart.

The evidence of this destruction was documented by Western Australian Museum divers in 1971. It consisted of fragmentation of major items such as cannon and anchors, together with many large boulders—weighing between one and two tons—filling the trench in which the mid-section of the ship lay. A number of unexploded charges were still in place around the wreck site (Henderson 1993:121; Kennedy 1998:34). Although small pockets of the site may likely remain undisturbed and reveal some information, its full archaeological potential will never be known. For a long time it was not possible to verify the identity of the wreck beyond doubt, although circumstantial evidence indicates that the site is indeed that of the *Trial* (Green 1977:44, 1986:204, 1997:426). At the same time as these destructive activities were occurring, there were some journalists and local divers among the recreational diving community who had the foresight and passion to seek protection for the old Dutch wrecks by using the press to argue against their destruction, and also to interest the community in their history (Henderson 1997:44).

Another Dutch wreck that has suffered significant human impact is the *Zuytdorp* (1712) off the Murchison coast (Henderson 1993:143; Peachey 2002). Reports of looting continue to surface today. Besides the HMA's *Sydney* and *Kormoran*, which are too deep for divers to access

Figure 2. Anchors scattered over what is believed to be the *Trial* (1622) wreck site, near the Monte Bello Islands (Photo: WA Museum).

(more than 2,000m below sea level), the *Zuytdorp* is the only shipwreck in Western Australia that has a protected zone surrounding its site primarily because of treacherous conditions (Figure 4) but also because of the extremely rare bullion that the vessel carried. This physical zone is imposed under the conditions of the Commonwealth Historic Shipwrecks Act 1976, and all vessels or individuals wanting to enter the zone require a permit. Despite treacherous conditions experienced at the site (conditions are often only calm enough to dive the site on two to five days in a year) and the difficulties of access because of its location (see Figure 3), it has been heavily souvenir-hunted. There have also been reports by historic shipwrecks inspectors, as late as 2009, that boats and abalone divers have been seen entering the zone at a time when no permits were issued. Unsubstantiated rumors by some recreational divers have also reached Western Australian Museum staff during this time about divers recovering coins from the *Zuytdorp* site. The remote location of the *Zuytdorp* makes it extremely difficult to monitor and police, and thus raises questions about the effectiveness of the Historic Shipwrecks Inspector Training program that each state and territory conducts under the commonwealth act.[2]

Figure 3. Divers having to rappel from the nearest cliff face and transport dive gear to access the *Zuytdorp* wreck (Photo: WA Museum).

Western Australia is, of course, not the only state where shipwrecks were subjected to random and deliberate disturbance and blasting. The *Catherine Adamson* (1857), *Catterthun* (1895), *Empire Gladstone* (1950) and *Dunbar* (1857) in New South Wales, to name a few, are among the many shipwrecks in New South Wales that suffered varying degrees of disturbances by souvenir hunters. These include random fossicking[3] and collecting to blasting of sites causing severe destruction, as in the case of the *Dunbar* (1857) (Robson 1994:20). One single diver collected in excess of 3,000 objects from the *Dunbar* over a 20-year period from the 1960s (see Figure 5). Over the years, he also gave away objects from his collection, telling others at the time not to reveal anything regarding it (Woodford 1993) for fear that authorities might confiscate it. It is difficult enough to access private collections for research and interpretation, but dispersals of relics from private collections, as in this case, create more complicated problems as it becomes even more difficult to trace movements of objects between individuals and results in the breakup of single collections and further loss of provenance and context.

The *Queen of Nations* (1881) located south of Sydney (4 km north of Wollongong) suffered a series of interferences and looting over a number

Figure 4. Treacherous conditions are common on the *Zuytdorp* site (Photo: WA Museum).

of years, with many early houses around the area reputedly built from timbers salvaged from this wreck (Smith 1992:9). Divers also used various tools to pry open wooden crates to access cargo items that were in mint condition despite resting underwater for 110 years. As well, the local council had forcibly removed sections of the wreck extending above the seabed because they considered them a hazard to shipping traffic (Nutley 2006:11). As a result of such activities, many objects have fallen into private hands, and the full volume of material removed from this and other wreck sites remain incalculable.

Shipwrecks in other states also suffered a similar fate. Wrecks in Victoria such as the *Clonmel* (1841), *Victoria Tower* (1869), *Loch Ard* (1878), *George Roper* (1883), *Light of the Age* (1868), and *William Salthouse* (1841) (see Figure 6)—just to name a few—all suffered from different methods and degrees of interference by private collectors and recreational divers (see, e.g., Anderson and Cahir 2003:177–178; Loney 1981). Wrecks in South Australia also experienced similar problems with sites being souvenir-hunted after government archaeologists or amateur historical society divers left a site after surveying it (Drew 2003). Nor were wrecks in Tasmania and Queensland spared from souvenir hunters and scrap-metal collectors.

Figure 5. Relics from the *Dunbar* on display at the Australian National Maritime Museum in Sydney (Photo: J. Rodrigues).

Legislation as the Immediate Answer

Efforts were made to halt the blasting and looting of the highly significant Dutch wrecks in Western Australia. In 1964, as a result of public pressure, the Western Australian Parliament modified the Museum Act to include protection of the Dutch shipwrecks and "the Cottesloe wreck" (the *Elizabeth*, wrecked in 1839). Responsibility for the act's implementation was given to the Western Australian Museum, but without adequate resources. In 1969, a new Museum Act was enacted, and the provisions for the 1964 amendments relating to historic wrecks were incorporated into the new act. In 1972, the ANCODS agreement was established between the Australian and Netherlands governments, relating to the management and care of the Dutch wrecks and associated relics. In 1973, the historic shipwrecks provisions were removed from the Museum Act 1969 and the State Maritime Archaeology Act was passed, incorporating a number of changes based on the museum's experience since 1964 (Kennedy 1998:32–33).

Figure 6. Part of a wooden cask lid from the *William Salthouse* in Victoria (Photo: J. Rodrigues).

The ability of the state of Western Australia to pass legislation relating to commonwealth waters was complicated by quarrels over sea jurisdictions and the subsequent passing of the Commonwealth Seas and Submerged Lands Act 1973. This was challenged successfully in the high court (*Robinson vs. the Western Australian Museum* 1976–1977 138 CLR 283) with the state act found to be invalid in this regard (Cassidy 1991:4; Kendall 1990:10). In 1976 the commonwealth government passed the Historic Shipwrecks Act 1976 to protect wrecks in commonwealth waters and honor its obligations under the ANCODS agreement. The scope of protection in this legislation was broader and included other colonial wrecks that were also historically and archaeologically important to Australia's heritage. Included in this legislation are both protection zones and the allowance of relic transfers between private individuals who had recovered material before legislation was passed.

The introduction of protected zones implemented a physical zone around a nominated wreck site whereby all forms of entry and/or interference with the site required a permit that listed specific conditions. Such zones are often used when substantial damage has been caused by looting, such as the *William Salthouse* (1841) in Victoria, or a site of dangerous nature where all diving should be discouraged such as the *Zuytdorp* (Hosty 1987:22), which also carried extremely rare silver coins. Sites of a sensitive nature such as the Japanese submarine off Darwin or those within Sydney Harbor could also be candidates for such zones. While there is good reason for imposing protected zones in these circumstances, placing protected zones over other wrecks for no rational reason could widen the gulf between divers and authorities and create a perception of distrust. Maritime archaeologists throughout Australia depend on the goodwill of divers and other members of the public in reporting wrecks as well as disturbances to wreck sites (McKinnon 1991:37), so such measures should always be considered very carefully.

It is likely that the Western Australian government felt the need to move quickly in proclaiming the commonwealth legislation to protect the Dutch wrecks that were being destroyed by vandals and recreational divers (Kendall 1990:10). The commonwealth government needed to enact protective legislation to honor its obligations under the 1972 ANCODS agreement but also to expand protection of Australia's underwater cultural heritage.

In 1984–1985, blanket protection, a concept that was created in preceding years, was introduced into the Historic Shipwrecks Act 1976 to automatically protect all wrecks in commonwealth waters that were 75 years and older from the time of wrecking. However, this was not enacted until April 1, 1993, a month before the amnesty was declared.[4] Once a wreck becomes historic, all relics associated with the wreck also become automatically protected at the same time regardless of their location. Anyone holding such relics—whether or not they legally own them—is obliged to declare their finds to the relevant state maritime cultural heritage agency. Before blanket protection came into effect, a long and tedious process was in place whereby a wreck deemed to be significant or suspected of being disturbed would be nominated for protection and had to meet certain criteria for legal protection. This process could take months, and in the interim, sites would be vulnerable to interference by divers, fishermen, and private collectors.

The legislation also allows for the custody transfer of relics as long as the custodian declared the relic within the stipulated time frame under the provisions of the act. In the first place, therefore, the relics must already be accompanied by a certificate that authorizes the custodian to keep them safely. To *transfer* custody of the relics (such as by sale or gift), the custodian must apply to the state agency for a permit distinct from the registration certificate. The objective of registering privately held relics and issuing permits for custody transfers is to have a record of privately held relics that enhances information about sites and the collections they produce. If the movements of privately held relics were regulated, state agencies would know the whereabouts of historic shipwreck relics in private hands. A problem arises, however, if a custodian moves or passes away without authorities being informed. In this case, the fate of a collection or object becomes unknown, and this is when the criticism of privately held relics is most justified because, over time, they potentially become lost from the public record.

Divers have a legal obligation under the commonwealth act to declare a newly discovered shipwreck, if they believe the wreck has not previously been found and reported (Hosty 1987:22). Provisions of monetary rewards were put in place in the act to encourage this, although it is generally accepted that some divers have not reported wreck sites to authorities (Hosty 1987:23). This reward system was essentially to replace the rights of divers that were lost because of the introduction of the Historic Shipwrecks Act 1976 (Hosty 1987:24). It is probably more an "award" of recognition, as some divers put in far more money, time, and effort to find a wreck than the reward can recompense. However, monetary rewards have not been given out for quite some time, as most state and territory agencies regard them as inappropriate. In addition, it causes confusion and animosity because of what divers see as inconsistent decisions about the amount of money allocated, which tends to depend on the significance of the reported site and value of cargo or bullion. There is also often disagreement between finders as to who found the wreck first and/or who officially reported it first.

Education

Maritime archaeologists at the Western Australian Museum (the first such unit to be established in Australia, in response to the discovery of the early Dutch wrecks) had recognized from the outset the need to train others to help manage and preserve the extensive shipwreck resources lying off the coast of the other states and territories. Thus, maritime archaeologists at the museum began teaching an evening course in 1980 in maritime archaeology in conjunction with the Western Australian Institute of Technology (now Curtin University) (Green 1989:218). Volunteer maritime archaeological associations also began to form in Western Australia and spread to other states. The years between 1976 and 1984 were marked by the gradual development of state-based maritime archaeology programs.

In the early 1980s, reports still emerged of pillaging and damage to wreck sites by explosives so that the development of these programs took an interesting form (Hosty 1987:23). A wreck would be discovered and threatened with looting. State legislation would be developed, and a maritime archaeology program established. State legislation would then be passed, and the commonwealth legislation proclaimed to operate in the waters adjacent to that state (Hosty and Stuart 1994:12). In addition, museum displays, publications, films, Web sites, databases as well as shipwreck and maritime heritage trails were developed to provide improved access for both divers and nondivers to be able to appreciate the historical and archaeological value of the sites. The community diver was also encouraged to participate in various projects around Australia on a state basis (Jeffery 1993:4). It is presumed that the Australian community will more readily identify with the historic shipwrecks program if they can see tangible results such as well-designed museum displays and popular publications.

Ultimately, the most effective means of giving back to the community information about their history, heritage, and identity—as well as obtaining their genuine support—must come from the efforts of archaeologists. Some collectors and divers, however, see the state agencies as iron-fisted authorities waiting to penalize anyone illegally withholding historic shipwreck relics. On the contrary, state agencies take a softer approach, such as allowing people to donate their illegally held relics (i.e., objects that were never declared during the amnesty or within 30 days of the wreck becoming historic under the legislation) and then treating this as a voluntary donation and acknowledging the donor's contribution, provided the person appears to have been genuinely ignorant of the law. Ultimately, it is the responsibility of both the public to be aware of and the archaeologist to inform the community about the laws and their obligations. Technically, however, anyone illegally holding relics is in breach of the act and could be prosecuted.

An Amnesty to Recover Lost Information

On May 1, 1993, a nationwide amnesty was declared in Australia under the Historic Shipwrecks Act 1976 and, initially, was to end on October 30, 1993. However, following numerous queries from fishermen, the commonwealth government decided to extend the amnesty for a further five months so that it finally ended on March 31, 1994. Although it provided people with more time to come forward and, thus, allowed for more material to be declared, there were disadvantages in declaring such a long amnesty (see Rodrigues 2009a).

Archaeological amnesties allow members of the public the opportunity to declare finds that they collected unaware of the law, ignoring the law, or when the status of finds has been altered because of changes to the law. The main aim of amnesties is to record information being held in private hands without public fear of prosecution. Amnesties are a way of filling gaps in the archaeological record by documenting the existence of souvenir-hunted artifacts, and this documentation can be greatly enhanced by the recording of associated oral histories.

The historic shipwrecks amnesty was declared to encourage divers and collectors with information about unrecorded wrecks or relics to come forward and give details without fear of penalty (Media Release 1993). The main objectives were to inventory artifacts that had been removed from historic shipwreck sites and had not been declared and to ensure that divers and collectors were not unfairly placed in breach of the act.

By the end of the amnesty, approximately 20,000 artifacts were declared by divers, private collectors, coin dealers, fishermen, schools, and small regional museums to which divers had donated shipwreck artifacts over the years. The collections include coins, glassware, ceramics, ships' bells, anchors, sheathing, alarm clocks, porthole scuttles, bolts, ballast stones and bricks, clay pipes, personal possessions, various ships' fittings, armaments, navigational instruments, and rigging-related artifacts, among others. These objects had never been previously recorded. A number of the items declared during the amnesty were also donated to the state agencies, but the vast majority were retained by the custodians, which was their right.

Not everyone who declared materials was the original diver or collector. Some had inherited them or declared them on behalf of institutions such as schools (Griffiths 1994; Southgate 1993). In addition, around 30 shipwrecks previously unknown to authorities were also reported. These were in a diverse range of locations (Cribb 1994), which provided insights into the accessibility of wrecks involved in the amnesty.

However, because the objects were opportunistically or intentionally claimed as souvenirs rather than archaeologically excavated, some maritime archaeologists feel that this renders the material meaningless because of site contamination, lack of contextual details, forgotten information, and uncertainty about provenance. This argument is valid only to a degree because research into samples of the amnesty collections have served to highlight the benefit of many of the objects, providing insights into the life of crew and passengers, the fashion of the time, the economic benefits of shipwrecks to remote coastal communities, vessel construction, cargo being transported, and even the wrecking events themselves (see, e.g., Ellis 2001; Fielding 2003; Knott 2001; McCarthy 2006; McPhee 2004; Philippou 2004). There is no doubt that souvenir-hunted artifacts always suffer from interpretation constraints due to the lack of contextual information or even deterioration over time; but if properly documented, these relics can reveal useful information about the site from which they came.

Regulating Private Collections: Does It Really Work?

As already mentioned, the Historic Shipwrecks Act 1976 allows for the transfer, sale, and disposal of historic shipwreck relics with a permit. Collectors and divers who had acquired artifacts from sites before legislation was introduced, as well as those who may have legally inherited relics, are allowed to keep them as long as they complied with the law and declared the relics within the stipulated time frame. However, the vast majority of custodians do not own the relics and, hence, are only custodians because it is the commonwealth government who owns these objects under the act.

The ability of collectors to retain historic shipwreck relics, or even sell or give them away, has been a bone of contention among maritime archaeologists in Australia. Today this can be seen as a breach of the 2001 UNESCO Convention on the Protection of the Underwater Cultural Heritage, although exception may be granted to objects collected before legislation was passed. To confiscate the relics would possibly mean that the Australian government would need to compensate collectors. If so, this is simply not feasible. Therefore, the relics remain in private custody, their ultimate fate uncertain. However, this matter was closely assessed again recently because of a case in Western Australia of a breach under the federal act, and it is possible that the commonwealth government, as the legal owners, are able to demand their return without compensation, particularly if the custodian has been convicted of a breach and is deemed unfit to care for the rest of his or her collection even if it was legally declared in the past. The reality is that unless a person applies for a permit or tries to sell the item (say, via eBay), authorities have no real way of policing the movements of historic shipwreck relics between individuals. As well, when collectors pass away, the fate of their collections is not known, unless they are a prominent figure and there is media coverage on the issue, such as in a recent case in South Australia (ABC News 2009).

Ultimately, while the idea of regulating private collections is to ensure authorities know their whereabouts and fate, and hence, the object is not lost to the public record, the reality is a very different story. Divers in Victoria and Western Australia have reported that pubs, cafes, and sailing clubs display undeclared relics from shipwreck sites. The number of attempted sales on eBay and police seizures of historic shipwreck relics is proof that the system has flaws (see Rodrigues 2010:1567–1568). For the system to work, collectors have to comply with the law and declare their items, yet not everyone does. Perhaps not enough advertising of the amnesty took place, or more efforts need to be made to educate the community about the laws protecting historic shipwrecks and associated relics and the legal implications resulting from the amnesty. The resolution is not simple. Custodians who have changed addresses or passed away make collections difficult to trace, and there is no guarantee the collections have not been disposed of by family members or the custodians themselves. The amnesty revealed a number of highly significant relics, such as a cutlass from the *Batavia* or cargo material and personal possessions from numerous shipwrecks, but some were also found in rubbish tips (Rodrigues 2009b:107). How many other relics ended up in rubbish tips or were never declared during the amnesty or how many sites have been looted since the amnesty took place is impossible to calculate.

Private collecting belongs to a world that is incompatible with archaeology and not as transparent. Most private collections remain just that—private. In theory, if everyone with historic shipwreck relics declared them during the amnesty, kept in touch with state agencies about the condition of the objects, updated their contact details, and applied for permits to transfer custody of the object, Australia would know where each relic is located and what is happening to it. This clearly is not the case. However, given that Australian authorities had no idea what response to expect from the public during the amnesty, it was not feasible to insist on surrendering all relics. Treating and storing so many objects requires long-term funding, storage/display space, and staff to manage the additional load. Given that privately collected material always has limited interpretive value because of lack of context or lost provenance, many archaeologists prefer not to deal with such collections. With such varied attitudes even from state archaeologists, the situation remains complicated. Is it better to forget about these collections, or should archaeologists try to recover as much information as possible for the benefit of enhancing knowledge and better interpreting sites and their formation processes before it is really too late?

Discussion

The moves made in Western Australia to protect shipwrecks, as well as its training programs to direct and contribute to the preservation of historic shipwrecks in other states and territories, had positive implications for the long-term stability of the sites. However, they also caused resentment with some in the diving community as their previous rights were now denied (Hosty 1987:21). Although the commonwealth Navigation Act 1912 required all finders of wrecks and relics to report these to the receiver of wrecks, this requirement did not necessarily protect the wrecks and was rarely enforced anyway. Protective shipwreck legislation, in fact, was always intended to curtail the activities of looting and souvenir-hunting but not to prevent divers, except in exceptional circumstances, from diving on the sites. On the contrary, it encourages divers who are interested in maritime history and archaeology to seek out the many wrecks that are still undiscovered. In addition, in the early 1990s, W. Jeffery (1993:2) suggested a rethink of the legislation, program, and future aims, given that it is likely the climate had changed from one of looting shipwrecks to one of giving greater protection to the environment, including cultural heritage material.

Australian maritime archaeologists had managed to create a strong community awareness of the need to protect historic shipwrecks, and

Australia has an enviable reputation in the areas of public programs, education, conservation, interpretation of historic shipwrecks, and legislative protection (Hosty and Stuart 1994:11). However, it has been 35 years since the commonwealth act was introduced, and 17 years since the amnesty ended, and divers are still interfering with shipwreck sites such as the *Zuytdorp* (1712) and also potentially the *Vergulde Draeck* (1656), and *Batavia* (1629) (see Rodrigues 2009c). More importantly, however, there is clear evidence that historic shipwreck relics are still being illegally held. Although the scale is likely to be much less than in the 1960s, the illegal collections still need to be dealt with appropriately so that the maximum volume of information can be documented. The vast majority of individuals with small collections or single objects that they donate to museums are treated sensitively so as not to give the impression that anyone in a similar situation will be prosecuted, because collectors are then more likely to covertly dispose of objects, which then become severed from public record.

Archaeological objects in private hands are always at risk of becoming lost from public record. Although the law forbids any transfer or disposal without a permit, policing the movement of relics in private custody is extremely difficult to do. The ultimate fate of private collections is always going to be a problem, and they are always under some form of threat (Henderson 1993:138). The commonwealth legislation has recently undergone a review and will likely be updated and made more relevant to the current climate and existing international conventions, but it is also very likely that the clause for relics transfer will remain because of legal complications. Thus, despite the moves in Australia to curtail further destruction of wreck sites, as well as to document and regulate the movement of private collections, there are still problems, and many of them are beyond the control of the state agencies. Education still appears to be the best approach to gain public support for preserving Australia's underwater cultural heritage; people tend to support a cause if they can understand the reasons behind it, appreciate its finite nature, and to see its value in the form of tangible results.

Conclusion

The full extent of damage that shipwrecks have suffered and how many relics remain in private hands remain incalculable. Australia adopted legislation, education, and an amnesty to protect its underwater cultural resources, and this approach has been largely successful, especially compared to those countries that have yet to protect their shipwrecks or are only just beginning to do so. However, close examination has shown that there are some flaws in terms of allowing the transfer of relics (which contradict basic archaeological principles), the lack of control over existing private collections, and the existence of collections that were never declared.

More and ongoing efforts need to be made to remind collectors and divers about their obligations under the act and to perhaps make it mandatory that this information is physically attached to objects so that, when collectors pass away, those who inherit their possessions or who have to deal with the estate will be aware of the laws relating to such collections. Some members of the public and archaeologists have informally suggested the need for another amnesty. While amnesties tend to defeat the purpose of having protective legislation, they do confirm suspicion that there are people holding on to relics illegally and are at risk of being prosecuted. This is further confirmed by the ongoing donations of historic shipwreck relics that are still transferred to museums and state agencies. Despite setbacks, Australia's approach in curtailing opportunistic and wholesale destruction of sites that occurred in the early years has been largely successful, especially considering funding constraints and the length of its coastline with the numerous islands where shipwrecks lie. State maritime archaeologists, divers, and politicians in the early years who contributed to significant moves in the 1960s and 1970s should be congratulated for their foresight in protecting shipwrecks for their historical and archaeological value—particularly the Western Australian government.

Acknowledgments. This research was mostly funded by a Postgraduate Research Grant (School of Social and Cultural Studies) and a Graduate Research Travel Grant, both from the University of Western Australia. Thanks to David Nutley for comments on an earlier draft and to Michael Gregg (Maritime History, Western Australian Museum) for subsequent feedback.

Notes

1. The agreement was executed on November 6, 1972 following a bilateral agreement between the Australian and Netherlands governments regarding the management, title, and care of the Dutch East India Company shipwrecks and their associated relics off the coast of Western Australia.

2. The Historic Shipwrecks Inspector Training is a program run by the maritime units of all state and territory agencies in conjunction with the Commonwealth Department of Sustainability, Environment, Water, Population and Communities to effectively increase policing of historic shipwreck sites. The program involves training field officers from other government departments (e.g., Fisheries, Department of Environment and Conservation, Water Police) to become inspectors under the Historic Shipwrecks Act 1976 and help monitor wreck sites and police unauthorized disturbances by divers and other members of the public.

3. *Fossicking* is an Australian term (of Cornish origin) for prospecting, with overtones of rummaging about.

4. For blanket protection (initially known as *blanket declaration*) to be in force, the act requires the minister to literally make such a declaration (i.e., announcing that all shipwrecks in Australian waters that are at least 75 years old are declared historic). In other words, it had to be gazetted. Essentially, the act gives the commonwealth minister the option (if he is requested to do so by the states and territories) to make the declaration. This amendment was introduced into the act but not declared at the time so that it could not be enforced, despite the fact that all state and territory agencies supported it (Rodrigues 2011:115). Clearly, the double level of state and federal administration makes such a process complex and time-consuming to put into effect.

7

The Trade in Fresh Supplies of Ancient Coins: Scale, Organization, and Politics

NATHAN T. ELKINS

When one speaks about the illicit trade in antiquities, images of Greek painted vases, marble and bronze statues, and an array of other "high art" objects immediately spring to mind. Media reports swirl around the return of high-profile antiquities with dubious collection histories to Italy and Greece. The trade in less-monumental objects (coins, fibulae, oil lamps, keys, jewelry, buckles, glass vessels, etc.) has historically received markedly less attention by scholars and the media, and yet the small objects trade is central to the wider trade in illicit antiquities. "Minor antiquities" often come from the same places as high art objects. A tomb containing frescoes and painted vases will also contain weaponry, less ornate vessels, coins, jewelry, or some other selection of material that the market would view as "less collectible" or "less artistic" (cf. Gill 2007b). The same applies to archaeological sites of various sorts where monumental inscriptions, mosaics, and statuary are commonly found alongside the objects of everyday life. Although we may naturally take more notice of the trade in high art objects, the "material and intellectual consequences" (a useful phrase coined by Chippindale and Gill 1993) of trading in fresh supplies of portable antiquities are equally severe.

Ancient coins have been the most widely collected antiquities since the Renaissance. Today their relative abundance and affordability, coupled with a widespread popular interest in collecting modern and world coins, makes them appealing to collectors. But irresponsible attitudes and practices in the sourcing of ancient coins contribute to the looting problem and therefore corrode the material record.

One of the first cases that brought serious attention to the unethical side of the trade in ancient coins was the Elmali Hoard that was found in Turkey in 1984, smuggled to Munich, and ultimately arrived in the United States. The two individuals who smuggled it out of Turkey were notorious antiquities traffickers based in Munich and were known to have ties to organized crime and drug trafficking (Acar 2001; Acar and Kaylan 1988; Fielder 1993). It is believed that the hoard from Lycia, valued at approximately $10 million on the American market, had well over 1,700 coins in it. It contained 14 Athenian dekadrachms, very valuable and desirable coin types to collectors. Most of the coins were returned to Turkey in 1999. Scholars published the hoard (see the relevant contributions in Carradice 1987); some results are necessarily speculative on account of the hoard's division and the lack of secure context. The case boldly illustrated the potential profits from illicitly trading in looted coins and also how commercial interests supersede scientific study and the preservation of historical information.

Some scholars have discussed the problems associated with an unregulated ancient coin trade more broadly, although the illicit trade in ancient coins has not yet entered the dialogue to a significant degree (for some comments and critiques—many by numismatists—see Beckmann 1998; Butcher and Gill 1990; Finley 1975:96; Göbl 1987:74–75; Kraay 1976:xxiv; von Kaenel 1994, 1995, 2009:22–23; Walker 1977; Wartenberg Kagan 2007). Although academics and museums have become increasingly sensitive to the effects of looting, and dealerships and auction houses specialized in other forms of antiquities have begun to establish guidelines and compliance departments (e.g., Sotheby's in light of Watson 1997) to avoid dealing in objects with dubious histories, a greater sensitivity in the market for portable antiquities has yet to develop. Therefore, it is useful to survey the role that the trade in fresh supplies of ancient coins plays in the antiquities market as a whole and to evaluate how the current lack of due diligence facilitates the sale of looted and smuggled coins.

Ancient Coins and the Antiquities Trade

In antiquity, coins were often produced in abundance and, in certain periods, were used by people of varying social backgrounds. As today, they were a facet of everyday life and are among the most common physical remnants of the past that have survived the ages. Second to potsherds, coins often comprise the majority of small finds at Greek and Roman archaeological sites. In the trade, common late Roman bronze coins can cost as little as 50 cents each when bought in bulk on Internet auction sites like eBay, while other coins have the potential to fetch millions of dollars at auction. To date, the record price paid for an ancient coin was two million Swiss francs (c. $1.75 million), exclusive of buyer's fee, for a Hadrianic sestertius struck from dies engraved by the "Alphaeus Master" (Numismatica Genevensis SA 5 [December 3, 2008], lot 233). This coin has a pedigree back to before 1975 when it was sold by Monnaies et Médailles as part of the S. Weintraub Collection (Monnaies et Médailles 52 [1975], lot 617 = Sotheby's New York 6043 [June 19, 1990], Nelson Bunker Hunt Collection I, lot 134). Even though they were objects of daily life, some coins have been transformed into most desirable and exotic objects by modern sensibilities and perspectives (cf. Vickers and Gill 1994:191–193 on Greek figure-painted pots; the price may also illustrate the increasing value of older pedigrees). Together with the fact that coins come from the same places as other antiquities, the potential riches that can be earned from smuggling coins makes the trade a fundamental and lucrative part of the wider market in fresh antiquities.

While hoards devoid of other associated features may supply the market with some coins, seizures of smuggler and looter caches demonstrate that the same people who loot to supply the antiquities market also loot ancient coins from archaeological sites. Scores of news reports are available to anyone with an Internet connection. Many of the reports frequently come from Bulgaria, one country whose rich heritage and history particularly suffers to supply market demand (e.g., Center for the Study of Democracy 2007:177–197).

Material and Intellectual Consequences of Dealing in Fresh Supplies of Ancient Coins

It is self-evident that unscientific prospecting for coins damages the archaeological and historical record in the sense that coins removed from archaeological sites and elsewhere will impair stratigraphy, disturb contexts, and that other objects will be removed in the process. The internal information from those hoards that may not be associated with other objects and archaeological features is also lost when they are broken up and sold without any record. But looting from archaeological sites and the dispersal of unrecorded hoards also negatively affects the study of numismatics itself (Beckmann 1998; Butcher and Gill 1990; Finley 1975:96; Göbl 1987:74–75; Kraay 1976:xxiv; von Kaenel 1994, 1995, 2009:22–23; Walker 1977; Wartenberg Kagan 2007).

Historiographically, numismatics has sometimes been an inward-looking and isolated discipline, much like the early study of Greek painted vases, with its own specialized methodologies and applications. Centuries of antiquarian study, collecting and classifying material, shaped the way these objects were approached and still exerts influence today (a useful and succinct historiographic summary is provided in Krmnicek 2009:48–52). Classification and systematization, methodologies handed down to us by the antiquarians, remain at the core of material sciences such as numismatics and archaeology. In the late-nineteenth and twentieth century, both numismatics and archaeology began to grow beyond their antiquarian beginnings, becoming increasingly self-aware, scientific, and interdisciplinary with a much greater focus on analysis and the writing of history (Finley 1975:87–100; Howgego 1995:xi–xii; Momigliano 1950; von Kaenel 1994, 1995). According to Hans-Markus von Kaenel (1994, 1995), two distinct currents in numismatic study can be traced back to the great *Wissenschaftsorganisator* Theodor Mommsen. On the one hand, he identifies a multidisciplinary approach that has developed in the tradition of Mommsen and, on the other, the persistence of a more inward-looking impulse. In his letter to accept the Medal of the Numismatic Society of London (now the Royal Numismatic Society), Mommsen himself appears to have differentiated between two streams in numismatic study:

> So I came to study numismatics. But very soon I saw that what I wanted was not to be found in a literature which, after Eckhel, has been left mostly to dilettanti and shopmen; and, as a young man and a rash one, I tried to write, myself, what I wanted to get written. I am fully aware that my numismatic works are far from satisfactory; nevertheless, they have contributed to bridge over the chasm between numismatics and history [Mommsen 1895; cf. comments also made by Göbl 1987:74].

This is not to say that Mommsen viewed the trade in a negative light. Rather, he thought that the study of numismatics was central to the study of ancient history when scholars were able to apply myriad types of evidence and methodologies instead of attending only to the coins themselves.

Ancient coins are material objects that are found alongside an array of diverse artifacts. To produce a more complete picture of the past, coins must be studied in multiple contexts and in conjunction with other disciplines. At archaeological sites, coins are associated with various occupation horizons and other finds on site (von Kaenel 2009 discusses the value of studying coin finds in close contexts, and Wigg-Wolf 2009 addresses series from a site as a whole). In addition to being one of the most important chronological indicators for archaeological sites, detailed study of coin finds has the potential to reveal other types of information (e.g., Sheedy and Papageorgiadou-Banis 1997; von Kaenel and Kemmers 2009). Intensive analyses at site-specific and regional levels can yield information regarding economic conditions, coin circulation and supply, demographic movement, military activity, and so on (e.g., Hopkins 1980; Kemmers 2006a, 2006b, 2009; Peter 2001; von Kaenel 1999, 2009; Wigg-Wolf 2009). At the stadium at Nemea, the coin finds of multiple city-states show from how far afield people came to watch the Nemean Games, and concentrations of coins from certain city-states in the seats illustrate the fact that spectators gathered in "cheering stands" as they do today (Miller 2004:109–110). The study of coins in archaeological contexts has also yielded information about ancient rituals (e.g., Haselgrove and Wigg-Wolf 2005). Contextual examination of the Roman necropolis and the associated coin finds at Avenches, for example, have indicated that certain reverse types were consciously selected and deemed more appropriate to be buried with the dead, as has Gorecki's study of Roman coins from burials between the Rhine, Mosel, and Somme (Gorecki 1975:266–274; Koening 1999:456–458).

Even in aspects of numismatics where it might not be so apparent, such as the study of coin iconography, attention to material context has proven its value in numismatics. There are recent indications from find evidence that the Roman state deliberately targeted certain populations with coins bearing images laden with ideological messages relevant to their station in society (see Kemmers 2006a:219–244 and discussion in Elkins 2009:42–46).

In addition to the disparate thousands of coin-find reports and inventories published in individual journals or excavation reports, several important corpora provide the groundwork for finds-based research. The best inventories come from the area of the former northwestern provinces of the Roman Empire, and especially the area of modern Germany. At the time of this writing, 41 volumes of *Die Fundmünzen der römischen Zeit in Deutschland* (FMRD) have been printed, cataloging a combined total of approximately 300,000 to 350,000 coins. The first volume of FMRD was published in 1960, but since then numerous other continental countries have initiated similar series. Other areas such as England and Wales have online finds databases, including the Portable Antiquities Scheme, which currently has recorded approximately 400,000 finds reported by metal detectorists (www.finds.org.uk). A large corpus of approximately 70,000 coin finds from Rome is being prepared for comprehensive publication; already the custodians of that data have frequently made the unpublished information available to numismatists for research.

The study of coin finds in archaeological context is important enough to warrant several different inventories to provide source material for comparative and regional studies. There is also an important monograph series dedicated wholly to the analysis of coins in material contexts: Studien zu Fundmünzen der Antike (SFMA).

In addition to the above-surveyed contextual applications within numismatics, the study of coin hoards are also important, especially for chronological purposes, and need not be from a specific context to be of some value. Nevertheless, even hoards that enter the market most often go unrecorded before they are dispersed and sold to various middlemen and dealers; both the contextual information and the potential internal value of the hoard are lost (e.g., Finley 1975:96; Kraay 1976:xxiv).

Certainly numismatics is a broad field that can be worked at from a number of perspectives that need not take account of material context in every case. However, the vast majority of fresh coins to enter the market will only add specimens of previously known and recorded types to our corpus and will, thus, contribute very little to numismatic science itself. In the rare instances when unique and unlisted coin types are found, what can be said about them is limited if it is not known from where they came and in what contexts and associations they were originally embedded (hoard or otherwise). Furthermore, invented histories of rare or unique coins that appear on the market are commonplace and can distort or mislead archaeological or numismatic research (e.g., see Fischer-Bossert 2008:15–17 on the effect of false provenances attributed to Athenian Dekadrachms).

The Scale and Organization of the Trade in Fresh Material

Fresh supplies of ancient coins easily make it to dealer inventories and ultimately to the hands of private collectors since there is little self-regulation in the market's present state. As regards the organization of the coin trade (at least those parts that are visible), there are essentially three classes of ancient coin dealers that can be distinguished:

1. Auction houses. These are often large businesses with many employees. Typically, ancient coin auction houses post six figure or million dollar prices realized after each auction, although they may deal in relatively small quantities of high quality and rare coins. In addition to periodic auctions they may host electronic auctions more frequently as well as electronic storefronts which easily cater to an international market.

2. Mid-range dealerships. These dealers operate independently or with only one or two additional employees or partners. Today, this class of dealer has a strong online presence, but may also conduct business at coin shows or physical storefronts. Their stocks are generally moderately priced, and they cater to the collector on an average budget.

3. Wholesalers. This class of dealership is often more closely connected to the procurement of fresh material and is therefore of greatest concern. Dealers in this class often import material in astonishing quantities directly from source countries and sometimes arrange for the smuggling of ancient coins and antiquities themselves. Other coin dealerships are the primary customers of wholesalers. Wholesalers sell their "better" material directly to dealers at "wholesale prices" and dispose of their "worse" or more "common" material directly to collectors over the Internet in bulk quantities.

Although most dealerships tend to have the primary characteristics of one of the above categories, it ought to be noted the classifications are not perfect. Auction houses and importers/wholesalers may have storefronts like a mid-range dealership, for example, and auction houses and mid-range dealers may organize the transport of material directly from suppliers in source countries.

Wholesalers supply many dealers and arrange for the import of material into the United States. The scale of their activities makes this class of dealership the one of most concern. A number of dealers operate in the United States who can be classified as "wholesalers," and many of them come from Southeastern Europe or the Middle East. A recently published report by the Center for the Study of Democracy (2007:186) about organized crime in Bulgaria estimates that between 30 and 50 Bulgarian nationals with residences in Western Europe and the United States operate as wholesalers and organize the bulk transport of looted coins and antiquities out of Bulgaria into these market nations. These individuals will wholesale their "higher quality" material to other dealers and normally dispose of their more common or less-collectable material en masse through eBay, VCoins, or other Internet platforms. According to the author's observations, eBay (USA) sees about 5,000 lots per week in the ancient coin section. This would result in between 260,000 and 280,000 lots per year. It is important to note that each lot may contain just one coin or thousands of coins, especially when wholesalers are selling uncleaned coins by the kilo or packages of 1,000 or more. Easily over 1,000,000 ancient coins are sold via eBay (USA) each year alone in the United States. This estimate excludes what will be sold through VCoins transactions, auction houses, and private-bid lists from mid-range dealers. When one considers that the largest and most important public numismatic collections in the world, such as the British Museum or American Numismatic Society, contain in the neighborhood of about 350,000 to 400,000 ancient coins at most, the size of the American trade alone is put into perspective.

One of the biggest wholesalers of ancient coins and antiquities in the United States in recent years is also a U.S. customs broker. This particular dealer has cleared other dealers through customs; he has assisted other dealers in importing material; and on online discussion lists, he has provided free advice on how to arrange for the import of ancient coins and antiquities while avoiding problems with customs. Much of this dealer's own stock comes from the Balkan and "Holy Land" regions. In a message from 2006, this dealer claimed to have a standing inventory of about 50,000 to 60,000 coins and that he sold approximately 15,000 coins per week in bulk and at wholesale (Chavarria 2006). According to online correspondence, it seems new supplies are always on their way to his inventory (e.g., Chavarria 2004).

In 1999, German customs officers seized a shipment of 60 kg of ancient coins (approximately 20,000 coins) at Frankfurt airport (Center for the Study of Democracy 2007:186; Dietrich 2002). The coins were falsely declared by a Bulgarian national living in New Jersey who operates as a wholesaler in the United States and supplies other dealers. Further research by German customs officials revealed that the individual in question had sent about one metric ton of material through the airport in previous weeks and months that had not been inspected. All of those shipments can be assumed to have been ancient coins and antiquities. If they were all ancient coins, the one metric ton that this single supplier spirited into the United States in just a matter of months would be about 350,000 ancient coins—a mass equivalent to the number of coins excavated and recorded through two centuries of German archaeology. Shortly after these shipments had arrived in the United States, there was much chatter on online ancient coin discussion lists about "a new source of ancient coins," naming the dealer personally and indicating that he actively supplied other dealers (e.g., see posts from an acquaintance of his: Burbules 1999a, 1999b). After the coins had been shipped through Frankfurt, he exhibited at a coin show in Chicago where he sold coins wholesale to other dealers and to collectors by weight. Were these coins that came from Bulgaria by way of Frankfurt? One collector reported:

> [The dealer/wholesaler] had a booth at CICF [The Chicago International Coin Fair] this year for the first time, and I had a chance to meet him. He wasn't retailing at his booth, he was strictly selling wholesale. I found myself drawn to his bags of late Roman bronze and bought them the only way I could – a handful at a time. Very pretty stuff. By mid afternoon of the second day of the show all his LRB [late Roman bronze coins] were gone. . . [Knapp 1999].

As of July 20, 2009, the wholesaler's eBay feedback ratings for his two seller IDs were 24,322 and 9,639. eBay feedback ratings are calculated by the number of transactions with unique user IDs, and so essentially, these numbers indicate the number of unique customers. Bulgarian authorities also suspect this individual may have been involved in a museum theft in Bulgaria in which numismatic objects were stolen (Center for the Study of Democracy 2007:186).

Some coins in the trade are naturally resold and "recycled," but fresh material—and there are massive quantities of it and great demand for it—come directly from source countries, especially in the Balkans and the Middle East.

Efforts to Protect the Status Quo

The Ancient Coin Collectors Guild (ACCG) was founded in 2004. The ACCG is a 501(c)4 organization to which donations are not tax deductible since up to 100 percent of its funds can be used for the purposes of political lobbying. According to its website, the group's objectives include three important points that are central to its activities:

- To lobby effectively against the imposition of import restrictions on coins of any age or place.

- To seek, in the event of adverse legislative action, favorable administrative or court interpretations affirming the right of individuals to collect objects from the past.

- To fight for the continued existence of a free market for all collector coins [Ancient Coin Collectors Guild 2004–2009a].

The ACCG's formal position is that it is anti-looting, but at the same time, it opposes any U.S. legislation that hinders the import of suspect material. The group does not believe that market nations or handlers of imported material in market nations should be responsive to any ethical or foreign legal concerns as regards the import and sale of fresh supplies of ancient material.

Although the lobby's titulature presumes a collector interest, it caters to a commercial interest in attempting to liberalize a market for ancient coins that takes no regard for the way in which new material enters it. The listed objectives illustrate this as does the fact that the biggest financial backers and supporters of the lobby's activities are not collectors but rather dealerships (cf. Gill 2009c). The highest class of membership is "benefactor," which requires a contribution of $5,000 or more. At the time of this writing, ten donors are listed in that category, and eight of them are dealerships. The vast majority of the ACCG's highest annual membership category, "patrons," who contribute at least $250 per year, are also dealers (Ancient Coin Collectors Guild 2004–2009b). Additionally, of the seven leading officers listed on the ACCG's website in 2009, all are dealers or closely involved with the trade (Ancient Coin Collectors Guild 2004–2009c).

The lobby is waging a public relations battle against calls for greater transparency and due diligence with regards to the antiquities market's effects on history, a battle most intensively waged on the Internet. Several editorials are posted on its website, but certain leaders of the group also maintain some rather pointed weblogs and rouse collectors on Internet discussion forums.

Accusations of conspiracies are endemic among some groups who feel threatened by increasing concern for greater ethical responsibility and transparency in the trading of antiquities. More than a decade before the founding of the ACCG, a review by Kevin Butcher and David Gill (1990:947) of the periodical *Minerva* noted:

> *Minerva*'s archaeologically responsible image has however been tarnished by an article by one of the Contributing Editors, Dr. Arnold R. Saslow. In an article entitled the "The Turkish connection; the ancient coin marketplace," Dr. Saslow discusses the role of Turkey in the modern numismatic market. Those Turks who are involved in the (illegal) sale of ancient coins to feed the "coin market" are described as "enterprising individuals". A Turkish investigative journalist, Özgen Acar, who uncovered the story behind the "Dekadrachm hoard," is cast in the role of "an agent of the Turkish government." Saslow, himself a dealer, attempts to reassure collectors who may be concerned that they might be forced to return part of their collection as follows:. . . .

Certain ACCG leaders have taken cues from Saslow—a patron of the ACCG—and have made similar statements alleging conspiracies and collusion between archaeologists with both American and foreign governments. The group's executive director, for example, is generally hostile to archaeology and academic numismatists and has also alleged that archaeology itself has been "hijacked by zealots" who simply conspire for a monopoly on studying the past (e.g., Sayles 2004, 2005, 2007a). In 2007, as the U.S. Department of State asked for a period of public comment on the request from Cyprus to renew import restrictions and include coins of Cypriot type, the ACCG founder mobilized a letter-writing campaign and automated fax service, but also targeted the American Numismatic Society (ANS), an organization with both strong scholarly and collector components, in an attempt to pressure it to adopt their position. The ANS executive director later made a balanced public response on the issue (Wartenberg Kagan 2007) while noting she had received a message entitled "Pearl Harbor of the Cultural Property War" and another message that asked her to "get SERIOUS before American numismatists experience their own 'holocaust' at the hands of these ivory tower fascists." She then asked individuals to drop the bellicose language and offered the ANS as a forum for reasoned dialogue. The ACCG's executive director immediately boasted responsibility for the first subject line, again using the "good vs. evil" imagery of World War II and alleging cabals:

> . . . I was personally chastised by the Editor and ANS Executive Director as being "bellicose". I suppose I should be flattered. In response to the U.S. State Department's furtive manipulation of the CPAC hearing on renewal of an agreement with Cyprus, I had made the statement publicly that their action might be considered "the Pearl Harbor of the Cultural Property War". That was apparently offensive to some. Today, the State Department not only affirmed my conclusion, they launched a major offensive against coin collectors. This is not "Pearl Harbor", this is "D-Day" for Cultural Property Nationalists. If that sounds bellicose, it ought to . . . [Sayles 2007b].

The chair of the ACCG's International Affairs Committee also alleged conspiracy theories. Shortly after the ACCG was formed, he attempted to recruit members on an online discussion list in a message entitled "Uncle Wayne Wants YOU" by comparing the concerns of archaeologists and conservationists to Hitler and the Holocaust:

> A lot of collectors have had the foresight to join the ACCG. EVERY collector ought to. Any collector who doesn't think this organization is necessary, who doesn't believe there is a real threat, who expects all of this to "blow over" while he/she collects unconcerned, is living in a fool's paradise.

> There were many thousands of Jews who stayed in Germany after the Nazis took power. They did not believe Hitler would actually do the crazy evil things he had been ranting about.
>
> Cultural property law is not Nazi fascism. Those advocating it are honorable, well intentioned people of high moral character, not homicidal maniacs. But their proposed laws really do threaten to become a Holocaust for collecting [Welsh 2004].

In 2007, shortly after the U.S. Department of State accepted Cyprus's request to include some ancient coins in the extension of the Memorandum of Understanding with regard to import restrictions on undocumented antiquities, he used similar imagery:

> ... If the AIA sent a squad of radical archaeologists to your house to seize your collection, in the process verbally abusing you as a moral cripple responsible for everything bad that is happening to archaeological sites, wouldn't you be mad as Hades? Wouldn't you be ready to fight? Well get ready to fight, because that is more or less what they intend to do, and actually are doing, one small step at a time. They really believe that private collecting is wrong by their standards of morality, and that all antiquities ought to be taken away from collectors and private museums who own them, to be stored in public institutions under the care and control of trained academics who are the only ones worthy of being entrusted with that responsibility.
>
> If collecting is not important enough to fight for, in the end (not so very distant, in my opinion) we WILL lose the right to collect. In the process we will also lose other even more important rights and freedoms. I'm already fighting as hard as I can [Welsh 2007].

His service to the ACCG was recently recognized by the ACCG's Exceptionally Meritorious Service Award (Ancient Coin Collectors Guild 2008).

On the face of it, distortion serves the purpose of maintaining the status quo while the unmeasured tenor serves to intimidate anyone who might dare voice differing views (cf. Brodie 2006). It would be easy to counter or even dismiss intemperate allegations, but it is perhaps more useful to ask why the "debate" has degraded to such a level and why so many average collectors have bought into or even propagated the notions and statements made by disgruntled sellers.

Whatever the intentions of those alleging complots and using a polarizing tenor, it must be acknowledged that the acceptance of these by some collectors may be a result of their feeling isolated from the issues that have ushered in increased ethical sensitivity in the acquisition of antiquities with little or no previous collecting history. They perceive these as a threat to their avocation. Many have aligned themselves with commercial elements that they believe will protect their interests better than archaeology or preservation. It is argued here that addressing this problem can both temper the debate and promote a greater sensitivity within the market by empowering collectors rather than suppliers and importers.

A Way Forward with Collectors

Although the dealer lobby and its more vocal leaders have a profound influence over the views of many American collectors, any progressive and positive change in the role that the indiscriminate market plays in looting will have to be addressed by the end consumer: the collector. U.S. and source country legislation concerning the trade of recently looted material would be useful in stemming the illicit trade and could be better advanced with collector support. The obstruction that the commercial lobby advances does not benefit collectors and ultimately may hurt them since a less palatable form of regulation may ultimately come from without if no regulation comes from within.

Surely none of us was motivated to become academics for the pay and neither were most collectors motivated to collect ancient coins for financial gain. We pursue our vocations and avocations out of a genuine passion for learning about the ancient world. In this we share common ground, and it is logical that we ought to be natural partners in combating the behaviors that would impair material history for economic gain.

Research on the effects of an indiscriminate market is useful and helps to call attention to the problem, but demand ultimately drives and reinforces the market. Therefore, it would be more productive to step up efforts to engage in a direct dialogue with collectors about law, ethics, and the consequences of an insensitive market. To curb the growing problem of looting and the dispersal of unrecorded hoards, archaeologists and academics must embrace collectors directly, circumventing other interests. In doing so, both sides would need to be prepared to make some compromises on their positions. With the masses of ancient coins on the market and the number of active collectors today, it would be both impossible and impractical to try to hold collectors to a circa-1970 provenance standard on acquisitions, a date increasingly adopted by institutional collections and advocated by archaeological professional groups like the Archaeological Institute of America (AIA). On the other hand, if collectors would say, "I have decided that I will not purchase anything that has not been documented as out of its source country before today" and hold themselves and the market to that standard, this would be a great start and would soon diminish the profitability of fresher material. The successful efforts of countries like Italy at recovering material looted since 1970 has reinforced that benchmark date, but due to their nature, most coins will be unaffected by these developments. In any case, repatriation is not the point. We must recognize that we cannot restore the contexts of coins looted in the 1970s, 1980s, or 1990s, and so our common goals ought to be diminishing the profitability and market for more recently looted and yet-to-be looted coins.

Many ancient coin collectors have a strong interest in proactively addressing the role that the demand of an indiscriminate market plays. One numismatist and collector recently outlined a photo-registry scheme that could be used as standard for buying and selling ancient coins and maintaining histories (Snible 2008). Naturally, the dealer lobby is opposed to such a scheme; this was voiced by the ACCG founder's response to it (Sayles 2008). Nevertheless, more and more scholar-collectors appear sympathetic to some basic market standards and regulation, desiring more transparency in the market, and clearly do not wish to be party to the systematic destruction of the past (e.g., Witschonke 2009 contra the statement in Sayles 2008 that the status quo is not destructive). There are many well-known and erudite collectors who are not motivated by a commercial interest, and it would serve our common cause to reach out directly to this group of collectors and engage them in a cordial and honest dialogue about the issues and the need for broad-ranging ethical codes and basic self-regulatory mechanisms in the market. Such a dialogue would be welcomed by many collectors. Basic regulatory steps may also benefit collectors by ultimately diminishing the danger of acquiring forgeries, since many ancient coin smugglers and market suppliers also pepper the market with increasingly sophisticated forgeries, as evidenced by the fact that dies for making fake coins are commonly seized along with caches of looted coins (e.g., ANSA 2007; Sofia News Agency 2008).

The ANS could perhaps serve as a forum and a venue where a plan can be launched that will satisfy ethical collectors as well as concerned archaeologists and academics, by organizing and seeking input from a broad range of representatives from archaeological and academic numismatic societies and from the general collector community. It would also be critical that archaeological professional societies such as the AIA, The American Schools of Oriental Research, and the Society for American Archaeology develop initiatives to work with collectors on these issues as part of their education and outreach programs or heritage protection programs. Too frequently, concerned archaeologists and groups have hastily characterized the interests of looters, smugglers, dealers, collectors, and museums as the same. Although there is a hard-line element within archaeology that decries any association with collectors or collecting institutions (e.g., Muscarella 2009), which also contributes to the polarization of the issues and the resulting lack of action, certainly more will be gained by maintaining a discourse and engaging and enabling those interests that are not motivated by financial gain. Painting all stakeholders outside of institutional archaeology with the same brush alienates sympathizers and conscientious collectors, potentially driving them to feel more at home with those groups that seek to profit from the free import of material.

The trade in ancient coins is an integral and fundamental part of the antiquities trade as a whole, and its enormous scale is a testament to the growing problem of looting and the resulting difficulties it causes for the numismatic and archaeological record. The current lack of regulation and due diligence in market practices combined with organized efforts to combat protective initiatives only exacerbate the problem and reinforce criminal structures in source countries. Of all stakeholders, collectors who do not have a professional financial interest in an unregulated market have the greatest potential for making progressive change by insisting on greater transparency and refusing to purchase suspect objects from suppliers. Archaeologists and numismatists must increase their dialogue with the public about these issues, but they should also reach out directly to collectors to seek their input on diminishing the antagonistic role that a free market in antiquities and ancient coins plays in the preservation of our past and to search for amicable solutions to the problems that the darker aspects of the trade cause for both collectors and material sciences.

Acknowledgments. I am grateful to Rick Witschonke, William E. Metcalf, Ute Wartenberg Kagan, Hans-Markus von Kaenel, and David Gill for their honest and critical commentary on the difficult and complex issues addressed in various incarnations of this essay. All ideas and opinions presented here are my own. Since the original writing of this article in 2009, there have been some new developments. In 2009, the ACCG staged the importation and detention of coins from Cyprus and China to demonstrate that import restrictions on coins are impractical and ought to be revoked. The judge found in favor of the government, but the ACCG has filed an appeal; that case is pending. The Memorandum of Understanding with Italy was recently extended and has been expanded to restrict certain early coins and monetary instruments that circulated primarily in Italy.

8

The Social and Political Consequences of Devotion to Biblical Artifacts

NEIL BRODIE and MORAG M. KERSEL

In May 2002, sensational headlines began to appear in the world's media. "The Earliest Known Archaeological Reference to Jesus" (Wilford 2002), "Burial Box May be That of Jesus' Brother" (Kalman 2009), and "Stunning New Evidence that Jesus Lived" (Govies 2002) were among the many. These headlines announced the appearance of a commonplace limestone burial box or ossuary from the first century CE bearing the Aramaic inscription "James, Son of Joseph, Brother of Jesus." An article in the glossy archaeological magazine *Biblical Archeology Review* (*BAR*) proclaimed: "After nearly 2,000 years, historical evidence for the existence of Jesus has come to light literally written in stone.... The container provides the only New Testament-era mention of the central figure of Christianity and is the first-ever archaeological discovery to corroborate biblical references to Jesus" (Lemaire 2002:24).

Initial attention to the spectacular find focused on the fact that it might constitute tangible proof of the biblical narratives. Most of the Western world was soon caught up in the "James, Brother of Jesus" frenzy, which culminated in November 2002 with a public display of the ossuary at Canada's premier cultural institution—Toronto's Royal Ontario Museum (ROM). The November exhibition of the ossuary in Toronto was purposefully timed to coincide with the annual meetings there of the Society of Biblical Literature (SBL), the American Academy of Religion (AAR), and the American Schools of Oriental Research (ASOR), which brought it together with an audience of experts in the same city. Epigraphers, New Testament scholars, and archaeologists all made the pilgrimage to the ROM to see the box. Discussions surrounding provenience (and by *provenience* we mean "archaeological findspot") were rare, even though there were conflicting stories about the ossuary's object biography—about how it came to be in the possession of the longtime Israeli antiquities collector Oded Golan and about why it had only recently surfaced. Yet, although little was said about provenience, the issue of authenticity soon provoked controversy. The ossuary itself is almost certainly genuine (ossuaries of that general type and date are commonly found in rock-cut chamber tombs in the vicinity of Jerusalem, and hundreds have been excavated [Gatehouse 2005: 31; Magness 2005]), but with nothing certain known of its archaeological findspot or associations, academic skepticism about its inscription began to mount, and the inevitable questions about authenticity followed.

In December 2004, Golan was arrested and charged with forging artifacts and illicit trafficking in artifacts under the 1978 Israeli Antiquities Law (Burleigh 2008:243–256). As of November 2011, the trial was ongoing, although reports indicated that the charges might be dropped because of conflicting expert testimony as to the authenticity of the inscription (Shanks 2009). Along with the James Ossuary inscription, numerous other objects were named in the indictments, including an inscribed ivory pomegranate said to be the only surviving artifact from the First Temple of Solomon, which had been on display for many years in the Israel Museum, and the Jehoash Tablet, a stone fragment inscribed in Hebrew-Phoenician script recording repairs to Solomon's Temple carried out by King Jehoash, corroborating a similar account in 2 Kings 12:1–6 and 12:11–17.

The authenticity and, thus, the historical integrity of these important biblical artifacts and their inscriptions has become the subject of much ongoing academic debate, but their exact nature and, thus, historicity is being determined by expert analysis alone. Epigraphers and linguists are studying the formal and grammatical properties of the inscriptions, and natural scientists are examining the physico-chemical properties of the materials and patinas. It is not obvious to us that any concerted effort has yet been made to establish the provenience of any of the artifacts, even though verifiable archaeological findspot remains the most reliable guarantor of authenticity. If we could know exactly where the artifacts were found, and the nature of their associated objects and architecture, we would be more fully assured of their authenticity, and the debate would be settled (we would also be better placed to situate these artifacts in their appropriate historical contexts). Thus, we wonder, if authenticity is the issue, and if provenience is the ultimate guarantor of authenticity, why it is that provenience is not the primary object of investigation? Why are epigraphers, archaeologists, and natural scientists lining up to offer their subjective opinions on the authenticity or otherwise of these artifacts, when there has not been any serious investigation of provenience?

As archaeologists, we find this absence of enquiry surprising, and we suspect it might reveal much about the social and cultural contexts of the artifacts' reception, and we think there might be political considerations too. That is why, in this essay, we want to ask, for inscribed biblical artifacts and for artifacts from the Holy Land more generally, why it is that issues of authenticity have come to overshadow and outweigh those of provenience, and we want also to determine what the social and political consequences of prioritizing authenticity over provenience might be. To answer these questions, we consider how archaeological artifacts are transformed into "relics," and how that transformation relates to their reception and consumption. At the very least, it entails spiritual and historical revaluations, and we go on to discuss how those revaluations have an economic outcome. Next, we consider some political ramifications and investigate how demand for these spiritually, historically, and economically charged relics might affect the historical and thus political landscape of Israel. Finally, we return to the ROM and reexamine the economic and ethical contexts of its decision to display the James Ossuary and consider what it might reveal about museum governance in the twenty-first century.

Authentic Experiences

Pious pilgrims have long gathered archaeological artifacts from the Holy Land as religious relics, and tourists continue to do so today. Gift shops in Jerusalem and other centers offer for sale ceramic oil lamps, coins, and other small artifacts (Kersel 2006:99–108). Imbued with sacred aura, these artifacts are seen as material facts testifying to the literal truth of the Bible, facts that can be witnessed and that are understood to embody a kind of ancient immediacy. At first sight, it might seem incongruous to consider these small quotidian artifacts as relics in the same way as artifacts that have a direct association with a biblically attested person or event, such as the James Ossuary or ivory pomegranate, but we are attracted to the idea that all these artifacts share a metonymic quality, in that they are all perceived to be pieces of the Holy Land—pieces of the past in the present through which the past can be experienced (Gordon 1986:141; Wharton 2006:22). Thus, while the James Ossuary, the ivory pomegranate, and Jehoash Tablet might be encountered in museums, and small artifacts might be bought in gift shops, what the objects have in common is that they are believed to have been manufactured and used in biblical times, a fact that endows them with a religious or spiritual aura for the owner or viewer.

An authentic experience of the past presupposes an authentic object. For any artifact to possess the necessary sacred aura, for it to be considered a true relic of the biblical past, it must be genuine. Or, at least, it must be believed to be genuine. Fakes or replicas will not do. During archaeological ethnographic research conducted in 2003–2004 as part of Morag M. Kersel's (2006) doctoral investigation into the managed antiquities market in Israel, tourists were interviewed about their acquisitions in licensed antiquities shops. In Israel, it is legal to buy and sell artifacts from pre-1978 collections, and licensed dealers have archaeological material readily available for sale (although most has probably only recently been looted). One tourist stated, "I was just in Syria and Lebanon where I saw a lot of interesting archaeological artifacts for sale, but I didn't buy them there because no one could give me a *Certificate of Authenticity*. I knew that in Israel if I purchased from a licensed shop I could get a certificate and then I would know that the artifacts were real" (Kersel 2006:119). Even though most certificates of authenticity are created by shop owners on their computers and photocopied for multiple uses, most tourists and collectors do believe that the copied certificate assures the authenticity of the purchased object, whether or not its archaeological findspot is stated. For most customers, knowing that something is from "the time of Jesus," as one tourist related, is enough to satisfy them, and there is no real need to know exactly where the object came from. Purchasers of biblical artifacts rarely examine, question, or reflect on actual archaeological origins unless they are specifically germane to the historical underpinnings of a piece. Questions like "Does it come from the 'time of Jesus'?" suffice when the answer is in the affirmative. The perception that the genuine artifact not only confirms the historicity of the Bible but also materially connects with biblical times satisfies the consumer. Complex historical reconstructions achieved through archaeological research are of no immediate concern and perhaps even thought to be irrelevant.

Tourists and collectors are not alone. In the epilogue of a special issue of the *Society for Biblical Literature Forum* on problematic artifacts from the Holy Land, Christopher Rollston and Andrew G. Vaughn (2005) state that "so intense was our desire to see and hold our religious heritage that it was not uncommon, even for people with archaeological training, to elevate such an object from the antiquities market to a status high or higher than objects found in controlled excavations," thus admitting that even professionals can be blinded by an object that appears to be reaffirming faith and offering a direct experience of the past. Thus, we would argue that this desire for an authentic spiritual encounter with the biblical past is one reason why the authenticity of the James Ossuary and other biblical artifacts is at issue, but provenience is ignored. For many people, faith-based approaches to the past are as relevant, important, or as satisfying as scientific (archaeological) ones. The spiritual value of these artifacts can be as important as their potential historical value.

Economic Realities

Scholars who work in the politically fraught subject area of Near Eastern studies have long sought a standpoint of political neutrality from which to conduct their research. Susan Pollock (2008) attributes this endeavor to a mistaken belief in scientific exceptionalism. We believe that a similar claim of exceptionalism could be made in relation to economics. Academics are rarely disposed to consider the economic outcomes of their studies, nor do they countenance the influence of money on their work. They believe that academic research proceeds outside the commercial domain (despite some very obvious reminders to the contrary, such as the 8 cm [3.25 in] high limestone lioness sold at Sotheby's New York for $57.2 million in 2007). Collectors and museum visitors concur, they do not want their spiritual or aesthetic experience tainted by the profanity of money. Nevertheless, despite the economic myopia of academics and much of the public, biblical artifacts can function both as capital and as commodities, and for those with a pecuniary disposition they can generate large sums of money.

The commodity value of one of these artifacts is best demonstrated by the case of the ivory pomegranate. The pomegranate was first noticed by epigrapher André Lemaire in an antiquities dealer's shop in Jerusalem in 1981, when he recognized that its inscription might identify it as a piece of ritual regalia from the First Temple of Solomon. The pomegranate is thought to have been sold soon after Lemaire noticed it (although before he published it) for something like $3,000. Once he had published his identification in 1983, the pomegranate's value sky-rocketed. In 1987, an anonymous donor allowed the Israel Museum to buy the piece for $550,000 (Burleigh 2008:16–17; Shanks 2005:62). This prodigious increase in price over a period of six years was entirely due to Lemaire's recategorization of the pomegranate from artifact to relic.[1]

Golan has not sold the James Ossuary since its original purchase, but people have drawn profit from it anyway. Again, Lemaire was involved. Golan first informed Lemaire of the ossuary in May 2002 and allowed him to inspect it two weeks later (Burleigh 2008:14–15; Gatehouse 2005:30). Lemaire recognized the possible biblical association of the inscription and asked Golan if he could publish it (Burleigh 2008:18). Lemaire also brought the ossuary to the attention of Hershel Shanks, who is proprietor of the Biblical Archaeology Society (BAS). Lemaire was consequently able to announce the ossuary as an authentic artifact in an "exclusive" article in the November/December 2002 issue of the BAS publication *BAR* (Lemaire 2002).

But if it is Lemaire who deserves credit for recognizing the biblical significance of the ossuary, it was Shanks who moved quickly to realize its commercial potential. By September 2002, he had assured himself of the ossuary's authenticity, and by October 10, 2002, when he contacted the ROM about the possibility of placing the ossuary on display, he had already sold the film rights to producer Simcha Jacobovici and arranged a book deal (Burleigh 2008:34–35; Gatehouse 2005:30). The exhibition lasted for six weeks from November 15, 2002 to January 5, 2003 and attracted 95,000 visitors. The ROM announced it had made a $270,000 profit, of which $28,000 went to Shanks (Gatehouse 2005:35). Shanks and Ben Witherington III were quick to follow up, publishing *The Brother of Jesus: The Dramatic Story and Meaning of the First Archaeological Link to Jesus and His Family* later in 2003 with an initial hardback print run of 75,000 copies followed by a paperback edition (Moreland 2009:74). The television documentary program *James: Brother of Jesus, Holy Relic or Hoax*, written, directed, and produced by Jacobovici, was screened on Easter Sunday 2003 (Jacobovici and Golubev 2004) in the United States and, altogether, shown in 80 countries (Moreland 2009:74). It was released on DVD in 2004. The commercial exploitation of the ossuary continued with Shanks maintaining coverage in *BAR*, and in 2008, another book *Unholy Business: A True Tale of*

Faith, Greed, and Forgery in the Holy Land was published, this time by author Nina Burleigh (2008) investigating the background to Golan's trial.

What, if any, money Golan made from these projects is not clear. Shanks claims that Golan has earned "not a penny" (Burleigh 2008:200). It is perhaps one of the ironies of the case that as the erstwhile owner of the ossuary, Golan has ended up facing criminal charges in court while others have profited in his stead. Perhaps his luck will change if he is acquitted or if the charges brought against him are dismissed. An acquittal would validate the authenticity of the ossuary's inscription together with Golan's ownership, and its sale value would presumably be significant. Lemaire, who seems to have set the commercial bandwagon rolling, was paid $1,000 by the BAS in 2002 in the form of a "travel scholarship" (Gatehouse 2005:35).

Money then, or the promise of money, might be another reason why provenience is often ignored. While provenience might establish beyond doubt the authenticity of an artifact, it might also call into question ownership and in so doing eliminate the potential for personal financial gain. If, for example, the James Ossuary was in fact excavated after 1978, it could be claimed as the legitimate property of either the state of Israel or the Palestinian Authority, depending on where it was found, an outcome inimical to the financial interests of Golan, the BAS, and its various business associates. Establishing its authenticity by expert consensus, even if it is a less reliable method, does not challenge those interests. The same argument applies to the small artifacts sold in gift shops. Authenticity is a necessary prerequisite for sale. Provenience—which if it is post-1978, is illegal—might simply precipitate seizure or arrest.

Political Contexts

So far, our discussion of biblical artifacts on the market has illustrated two things. First, that perceived authenticity is necessary for spiritual engagement with a historico-religious object or relic. Many Judeo-Christian people seek a non-intellectualized experience of the biblical past through spiritual engagement, and authentic archaeological artifacts fulfill this role by offering a piece of the past in the present—a tangible memory. Knowledge of provenience is not important for this experience, but assurance of authenticity is. Second, we have demonstrated that people are making good money satisfying this public appetite for relics. It is tempting to view the arrangement as a harmless one—wily operators making money out of people who can afford to pay, or unscrupulous forgers scamming unprincipled collectors—and to leave the study there. Unfortunately, we do not believe that the study can be left there, as the beliefs and actions described exist in and are constitutive of a political context. Popular engagement with a perceived past presupposes a historical consciousness, and historical consciousness is a necessary aspect of social or political identity. In the presently fractured terrain of Israeli politics, material expressions of identity are expressions of power, in this case, socioeconomic power. To pretend otherwise would be an egregious example of the scientific exceptionalism critiqued by Pollock (2008).

Historical consciousness is forged at the nexus of history, memory, and imagination, and social theorists have talked about this consciousness being realized as "tradition" or "collective memory." Although these terms have been used interchangeably in the literature, we propose here an analytical distinction between "tradition," which we consider to be an officially sanctioned narrative or discourse, and "collective memory," which we believe to be its more demotic counterpart. We understand this distinction is overdrawn and are aware that official and unofficial narratives draw on each other, but for our present purpose the distinction is a useful one. "Inventions of tradition" are a well-documented hegemonic means of enforcing social identity or increasing social cohesion through historical affirmation (Hobsbawm and Ranger 1983), and more than one scholar has argued in this vein that the practice of archaeology in Palestine and Israel has been actively instrumental in implementing the British colonial vision of a Holy Land and the later Zionist project of an Israeli nation-state (Abu El-Haj 2001; Scham 2009; Zerubavel 1995). These successive, though intertwined, religious and nationalist discourses were made more "real" outside the textual authority of the Bible through the agency of "scientific" fieldwork and research, which fashioned archaeological sites into tangible reference points for biblical validation and commemoration. Museums were not exempt from these projects (Azoulay 1994). But although the materiality of official tradition might be fashioned by archaeological practice, the narratives it helps compose are only credible when they are present in a more primitive or less organized form in the collective memory of the social group concerned (Halbwachs 1992:120–166). Yael Zerubavel (1995:3) has defined collective memory as "the history that common people carry around in their heads," and for our purposes we are interested in the histories carried in the heads of people who visit the antiquities shops and museums of Tel Aviv and Jerusalem and in places further afield such as Toronto.

Tourism is an increasingly important component of the Israeli economy, and publicly at least, it has forced more plural interpretations onto the public presentation of archaeological sites, which are intended to accommodate although not necessarily reconcile the various Jewish and Christian narratives and beliefs of site visitors (Bauman 2004; Silberman 1997). Nevertheless, this plural past is still a selective one, sanctified and legitimized by the authority of the Bible (Abu El-Haj 2001:237–238; Shavit 1997:61). The Islamic narratives of Palestinian or other groups are neglected or intentionally excluded (Bauman 2004). The past that sells at the admission kiosk is the one that is offered for public consumption, and for the time being, at least in Israel, not many people are buying the Islamic past. We suggest that this commercially driven reification of collective memories applies as much to artifacts as it does to sites.

As we described above, there is a strand of modern-day tourism in Israel that can be traced back to the medieval devotion of pilgrimage, and like the pilgrims, modern-day tourists like to view or to own sacred relics such as the ones discussed here. Together with the constituencies of museums such as the ROM, they constitute a selective demand, both for particular types of artifacts and for the particular beliefs and histories that those artifacts help constitute. According to the Israel Antiquities Authority (IAA) in 2009, for example, the material most in demand on the market has in the past comprised Jewish and Christian coins and artifacts, and it is only recently that Islamic artifacts have started to join them.[2] This preferential demand for Jewish and Christian artifacts has been noticed before. In 1992, it was reported that "Jewish" coins were more valuable on the market than "Arab" ones (Abu El-Haj 2001:255), and during Kersel's (2006:66) doctoral research, an IAA interviewee expressed his/her opinion that the looters knew there was "more money to be made from artifacts with a Jewish or Israeli connection." This customer preference was highlighted by an incident in a West Jerusalem antiquities shop catering to an elite tourist base (Kersel 2006:120). During a visit to the shop, on King David Street, an expert in Islamic ceramics noticed that an Islamic piece was mislabeled as "Herodian" (another way of saying "from the time of Jesus"). The mistake was pointed out to the proprietor, who responded, "Oh I know, but Herodian sells better, and it's all about customer satisfaction." The lamp, while labeled incorrectly, is genuine, and the customers are being offered what they demand—an artifact from the time of Jesus. These same tourists no doubt visit archaeological sites and would queue up in museums to view artifacts such as the James Ossuary and the Jehoash Tablet.

When artifacts undergo the spiritual revaluations that are necessary for their transformation into relics, they are rendered accessible to the collective memory as tangible facts of narrative history, and when this collectively remembered history reinforces or underwrites an official version of political legitimacy, as it does with the Jewish claim to Israel and the concordant Christian tradition of a Holy Land, then these same artifacts as relics also become charged with political significance. Those who decide what artifacts are valuable also decide what history is valuable. Thus, although the market in Israeli antiquities is to all appearances politically disinterested, driven as it is by faith and commerce, it might still have political outcomes. Demand places a monetary value on artifacts, and that monetary value causes them to be illegally excavated or faked, and then passed onto the market, whence they enter museums, private collections, the academic literature, and ultimately the public and political consciousness, as the material confirmation of history. Whether small bronze coins from the time of Bar Kochba or an inscribed ossuary from the time of Jesus, they "concretize" history, but it is a specific, Judaeo-Christian history. Islamic artifacts are not encouraged to "appear" in the same way. Christians and Jews do not buy them, so they are worth less than their Judaeo-Christian equivalents, and there is no real monetary incentive to fake them or to dig them up. Islamic history is not concretized. The market in holy artifacts may not in itself be discriminatory, but the consumers are, and through their cumulative acts of acquisition and devotion, they encourage the materialization of one historical narrative at the expense of another. *So what is your point?*

Museum Ethics

In Byron McCane's (2009:20) discussion of the James Ossuary, he asserts that "an artifact with no known archaeological context or provenance was presented to the SBL and to ASOR by persons with no scholarly credentials or academic affiliations." We might ask how this can have happened, particularly, as McCane continued, the same persons "stood to profit substantially by displaying the artifact," as we have shown. Prior to the ossuary's display at the ROM, Shanks had obtained private assessments of its inscription's authenticity from Lemaire and the Geological Survey of Israel (Burleigh 2008:34–35; Gatehouse 2005:30), but the ROM did not subject it to rigorous and transparent academic scrutiny and scientific testing or even an assessment by the Israeli governmental body—the IAA—charged with the oversight of artifacts of national importance. Nor, crucially, did it establish provenience. "Due diligence" of this sort is standard museum practice, but in this case, it appears not to have happened. McCane suggests—and all the published evidence supports him—that economic considerations were paramount for the exhibition broker (Shanks) and, more importantly, for the ROM itself. Led astray by the lure of the profit margin and the possibility of material verification of the existence of Jesus, they ignored the skeptics.

The role of the ROM in this affair deserves more than a little attention. In many ways, a museum acts as a gatekeeper, occupying a position that allows it to decide what artifacts should be accepted as culturally important and on what grounds they should be accepted. The public invests authority in the museum for that purpose and expects in return that the museum should be diligent in its practice. As museum professionals are keen to emphasize, museums enjoy the public trust (Cuno 2004). By the time an artifact is presented at exhibition as genuine, the public expects that all necessary checks have been performed by the appropriate experts. By prematurely and perhaps mistakenly presenting the ossuary as genuine, the ROM failed in its gatekeeping duty—it opened the gate to a man brandishing dollar bills without first conducting the necessary baggage inspection.

But this characterization might be treating the ROM unfairly. The reality of the situation is more complex. In displaying the James Ossuary, the ROM took on several roles at once. It became the custodian of a sacred relic, a suspected collaborator in the illegal trade in antiquities, a shaper of public interpretation, a fiduciary institution, and the promoter of a saleable item. Not surprisingly, this mixing of roles was confusing, sometimes contradictory, and ultimately perhaps damaging to the museum's mandate of public service. It exposed very publicly a discordance between different strands of the ROM's mission—between obligations to the material curated and obligations to the museum's public.

The strategic objectives of the ROM's mission are available online.[3] They include the following:

- To produce nationally and internationally outstanding and innovative programs of agreed research and collections management.

- To use the highest ethical standards in all aspects of museum operations, including human resource management, and to have policies which are understandable, meaningful, and consistently and fairly applied.

These objectives might be characterized as expressing the ROM's obligation to curated material. The ROM undertakes to acquire, curate, and research material to the highest applicable standards. But the strategic objectives also include the following:

- To exceed visitor expectations for engagement and a meaningful experience.

- To produce surpluses to fund operations and aspirations as defined in business plans, while increasing the proportion of self-generated revenues each year.

These objectives express a different aspect of the ROM's mission and establish its obligation to the public that supports it. Both of these mission obligations are laudable, but in the case of the James Ossuary, they came into collision.

ROM press releases issued at the time of the exhibition (ROM 2002a, 2002b, 2002c) clearly expose the dilemma posed by the ossuary to its strategic objectives. The press releases were keen to emphasize that the ROM was the first museum to display "the world-famous James Ossuary, which has been described as the most important find in the history of New Testament archaeology" (ROM 2002c), but they were also careful to introduce an element of scholarly doubt and caution, promising to "bring forward the various expert theories regarding its religious significance and archaeological history" and to present "a balanced view of some scholars' recent, and to some, controversial claims about the container's authenticity, history and meaning, from both the scientific and social perspectives." Supporting material on display at the exhibition espoused similar themes (Bremer 2009). This intention to explore controversy fits well with the strategic objectives of promoting meaningful visitor engagement and increasing self-generated revenue. But it would only be possible by abandoning another objective, the desire to operate according to the highest ethical standards.

The amended 2001 ROM policy on ethics and conduct states that all employees must:

> ... observe the principles established by the Canadian Museum Association's Ethics Guidelines (1999) and the International Council of Museums' (ICOM) Code of Ethics (revised edition, 2001) [Royal Ontario Museum 2001].

As regards unprovenienced archaeological artifacts, the 1999 Ethics Guidelines of the Canadian Museums Association are not very specific. Article E states:

> Museums should be particularly conscious that material acquired in an illicit, unethical or exploitative manner may be offered for donation, loan, or identification. They should therefore develop procedures to avoid such situations [Canadian Museum Association 1999].

But at the time of the exhibition, the ICOM ethics were explicit and offered the highest ethical standard. According to the then-current 1986 ICOM code, a museum should not accept excavated material on loan:

> ... where the governing body or responsible officer has reasonable cause to believe that their recovery involved the recent unscientific or intentional destruction or damage of ancient monuments or archaeological sites, or involved a failure to disclose the finds to the owner or occupier of the land, or to the proper legal or governmental authorities [ICOM 1986].

In short, the ROM should not have acquired the ossuary on loan without an adequate account of provenience. Without such an account, it was not acting according to the highest ethical standard (ICOM's) as required by its own strategic objective.

In July 2003, in a further press release issued in response to police questioning of Golan, the ROM stood by its assessment of the ossuary's authenticity and emphasized again that the museum existed in part ". . . to help facilitate public understanding and debate about important artifacts and specimens" (Royal Ontario Museum 2003). Finally, and damningly perhaps, it also admitted that the provenience was unknown: "There is always a question of authenticity when objects do not come from a controlled archaeological excavation, as is the case with the James Ossuary" (Royal Ontario Museum 2003). In response to a letter written to the ROM's director, William Thorsell, in June 2004 about this issue of unknown provenience, he replied that the ROM had held discussions with the IAA over the loan of the ossuary and that the IAA had licensed its export.[4] When agreeing to the loan, however, the IAA "had no idea" of the ossuary's potential importance as Golan had not mentioned the inscription (Burleigh 2008:57; Gatehouse 2005:30). Furthermore, in his letter, the ROM's director also expressed the ROM's belief that the ossuary had been acquired on a legal market 40 years before the date of exhibition. If this had been true, it would have placed the ossuary outside the qualifying "recent" stricture of the ICOM code. But the ROM's only source of information in this matter would have been Golan himself. The ROM must have taken his word at face value, without any material verification, which is not acceptable due diligence. Since the ROM display, the only evidence of ownership history that Golan has produced comprises photographs of the ossuary in his home dated to 1976 (Barkat 2007). Critically, the date 1976 is later than the 1970 threshold established by the *UNESCO Convention on the Means of Prohibiting and Preventing the Illicit Import, Export, and Transfer of Ownership of Cultural Property*, which has now been generally accepted by the international museum community as the point of demarcation between "recent" and "past" episodes of illegal or destructive misappropriation of cultural objects (Brodie and Renfrew 2005:351–353). The ICOM ethics spoke of "reasonable cause to believe," and although provenience is not known, as the ROM itself admitted, and the ossuary's history is not known before 1976, there will always be reasonable cause to believe that its excavation involved the recent unscientific or intentional destruction or damage of ancient monuments or archaeological sites, and therefore its acquisition or loan should be avoided. This was the ethical standard set by ICOM, and it was the standard that the ROM failed to meet.

When faced by the James Ossuary, the ROM was placed in the unenviable position of weighing the ethical cost of displaying a newly surfaced object of unknown provenience and not yet vetted by the academic and scientific communities against the museum's obligation to the public—presenting visitors with the opportunity to view an astonishing find in the history of archaeology. For its income, the ROM is dependent on direct public support, private benefaction, gate receipts, and other visitor expenditure. At a time when the ROM's direct public support was being reduced, the ossuary was a "god send" (pun intended) for making good the economic shortfall by increasing visitor-related revenues. Even then, it appears that the ROM did want to assess the ossuary properly before agreeing to an exhibition, until Shanks threatened to offer the ossuary instead to the Metropolitan Museum in New York or the Smithsonian Institution in Washington, D.C. (Gatehouse 2005:30). This threat placed pressure on the ROM to act quickly or lose the financial boost of exhibiting the "find of the century." The ROM's hand was further forced when Shanks announced at the October press conference unveiling the ossuary that it would be displayed at the museum to coincide with the SBL and ASOR meetings in Toronto (Gatehouse 2005:30). The pressure to capitalize on the economic potential of the ossuary may have encouraged the museum staff to be less critical of the issue of the authenticity and less cognizant of ICOM's ethical advice. For the ROM, then, a discordant mission allowed or forced them to choose between an ethical and a profitable course of action. It chose the latter, but in so doing set in train a sequence of events that ultimately brought its reputation into question—a reputation that museum ethics are designed to protect.

The attitudes of museums toward unprovenienced objects (that are acquired on loan or through bequests, donations, or direct purchase) are often in a state of flux. While ostensibly adhering to civic-minded mandates for public engagement, museums can easily embrace an object as a relic, a treasure, or a work of art, or less publicly, as a visitor attraction or a means of exhibiting prowess in the marketplace or of overshadowing rival institutions. Their willingness in these circumstances to turn a blind eye to issues of provenience ensures that the demand for looted artifacts persists. It also ensures that sometimes, perhaps often, objects that are fake, as might turn out to be the case with the James Ossuary, meet this demand. But when the museum itself is arbiter and guarantor of authenticity, if it displays a forged object as genuine without first conducting the appropriate due diligence, it betrays itself, and it betrays the public trust. The lie, as Oscar Muscarella (2000) has said, becomes great.

Conclusion

It is a long way from a rock-cut tomb outside Jerusalem to a gallery inside the ROM, and there are conceptual and physical distances, too, between territorial claims in Israel and museum governance in Canada. Bruno Latour (1993) would recognize these observations as signs of a hybrid network, of people acting on objects and objects acting on people over distance. Latour would also resist reduction to the sociology of Pierre Bourdieu (1984), but it is hard not to recognize the multiple exchanges of economic and various forms of cultural capital that are in play. The scandal of the burial box has exposed more of the antiquities trade network than would normally be the case, and we have offered only a preliminary sketch of its lineaments. We hope, however, to have done enough to demonstrate the wide-ranging social and political circumstances and consequences of the trade in biblical artifacts.

Acknowledgments. David Gill and Christopher Chippindale will recognize that we have appropriated their unforgettable phrase for our title. We hope they don't think we have misappropriated it.

Notes

1. The effect on price of Lemaire's identification highlights the positive impact of scholarly work on the antiquities trade.

2. Electronic document, http://www.antiquities.org.il/shod_eng.asp, accessed November 21, 2011.

3. Electronic document, http://www.rom.on.ca/about/pdf/boardpolicies/vision.pdf, accessed November 21, 2011.

4. Letter dated June 15, 2004, written by ROM director William Thorsell in response to a letter written by Neil Brodie on May 20, 2004.

9

What All the King's Horses *Has to Say to American Archaeologists*

ANN M. EARLY

During the late 1970s and 1980s, grave-digging and the sale of artifacts from Native American sites surged in Arkansas and neighboring states where I carried out my research. Fueled by a new group of wealthy collectors, increased regional- and national-level merchandizing, and the in-state efforts of several commercial dealers, and as yet unrestrained by unmarked grave protection laws, the digging ranged from old-fashioned probe-and-shovel expeditions to backhoe and bulldozer assaults on mounds that had somehow escaped several earlier episodes of relic hunting that took place in the previous century.

Some wealthy and socially connected collectors laid claim to the ennobling nature of their actions by promoting and facilitating a public exhibit of Arkansas Native American pottery at the state's principal arts center. All of the objects, so far as we archeologists could tell, were from looted contexts, and virtually all were loaned by private collectors and small private museums. Provenance, condition, estimated age, and current ownership information were withheld in both the exhibit and the accompanying catalog, leaving archaeologists to rely on our (not inconsiderable) personal knowledge and the common gossip pool to estimate source sites and current owners. This was in an era when "I'll show you my prize, but I won't tell you where I got it" was a common refrain from both diggers and collectors. Today, a great many of these objects appear to have moved on to other owners or to have disappeared from view.

In addition to arranging the exhibit of their own artifacts and those of other people in their collecting network in the state's highest status arts venue, two collectors laid their claim to personal connoisseurship as well as possession by organizing and writing a locally published exhibit catalog. The then–survey director, Charles R. McGimsey, and state archeologist, Hester A. Davis, were invited to insert brief, sidebar, capsule statements about the state's prehistoric time line, the history of archaeological work, and a single-page statement about the importance of context. The chapters about the pottery articulate the collectors' worldview, innocent of any reference to the work of scholars active in the last century, regarding Native American culture, technology, and aesthetics as well as symbolic referents and purpose of the artifacts. Personally, I found the Mississippian "Breast Effigy" most evocative of this approach (Westbrook and McEntire 1982:35). Individually, nearly all objects in the exhibit seemed to be unblemished examples of Native American manufacture, although a few seemed "wrong" to me in comparison with the several thousand vessels I had observed closely by that time. Some lacked the weathering associated with 500 years of burial; others had configurations that were not found in extant photo files and publications.

At about the same time, I visited a member of the collectors' group to meet him and view his collection. He showed me one item that he was particularly fond of: a shallow, engraved bowl. A small, spherical, stylized anthropomorphic head was mounted on the rim. The head was hollow and contained small pebbles that rattled when the bowl was shaken. These "rattle bowls" with one or two heads opposing each other on the rim are well documented in southwest Arkansas collections. My host commented that since he did not have one of these in his collection, he had his restorer implant a head from someone's potsherd collection onto a plain bowl already in his collection, thus creating an object that, by all appearances, was a genuine rattle bowl.

Professional restorers who cater to collectors are tasked with repairing broken objects and rendering the breaks, missing pieces, and other flaws invisible. They may also be called on to "improve" a piece, as in the case of the rattle bowl. As a result, the rattle bowl, like most objects that circulate in and out of private collections, showed no signs of its "married" status, to borrow a term frequently applied in the antique furniture trade to refer to objects assembled from once-separate parts.

This "new" rattle bowl story is nothing new to those archaeologists who still work extensively with material culture. It is emblematic, however, of artifacts sold and exhibited in collections stocked through the antiquities trade that display the varying degrees of fakery and untrustworthy context that infect these collections and threaten the integrity of any research that draws on such objects.

The essays in this collection reveal many of the ways that both scholars and the public are deceived as a result of the antiquities trade. For scholars, corruption of the essential material base for studies and interpretations, whether by fakery or misattribution, leads to fanciful or outright fictional narratives about people and cultures that block honest scholarship and waste both research monies and scholars' lives. Since public interpretations lag behind actual scholarship, inaccurate stories about past people and cultures may linger a generation or more in exhibits, visual media, popular books, and educational materials.

In addition to the corruption of information, looting is a common thread in most of these presentations. We cannot separate looting and site destruction from the subject of antiquities trafficking, and numerous books, articles, watchdog columns in journals, and other outlets have made the connection clear in the last several decades.

Another important structural thread in any discussion of trafficking is fakery. The articles in this volume by Senta C. German on Minoan and Mycenaean artifacts and by Neil Brodie and Morag M. Kersel regarding some high-profile Holy Land artifacts and issues of authenticity both focus on embellishment and fakery, and the powerful consequences they have for both contemporary people and the constructed history that we dispense. Deliberate, or even unintended fakery, if not the gorilla in the room at any discussion of looting, is surely a very large chimpanzee. This may be because most archaeologists who do not believe themselves directly affected by site and artifact loss do not spend much time thinking seriously about either. Some studies indicate that fakery is far more prevalent than the average person's wildest imagination, and if we were to devote more time to documentation and quantification of the practice, that gorilla may morph into an elephant.

This Volume and Americanist Archaeologists

All of the essays in this volume, and the majority of literature dealing with illicit antiquities and looting, deal with Old World sites, cultures, and objects. That comes as no surprise when high-end antiquities from Old World sites, some commanding million dollar price tags in recent decades, make international news and serve as poster children in debates about looting, smuggling, fakery, and issues of cultural patrimony. There is, further, a diverse community of constituent groups with vested interests in these antiquities. It includes archaeologists, art historians, museum curators and directors, wealthy patrons, academic historians, tourism and cultural heritage professionals, religious zealots, and politicians as well as diggers, smugglers, dealers, wealthy collectors, drug lords, and members of the interested (and culturally prideful) public. This does not mean that looting or antiquities trafficking is worse, but it is complex and high profile. There have been more people studying and reporting about the issues as they apply to Old World situations as well.

Archaeologists working in the Americas are aware that looting and antiquities trafficking take place in their domain, but the degree of popular awareness, the range of constituencies concerned with the issue, and the decibel level of alarm about the situation all appear less. Those situations where the endangered sites and cultures can be considered the contemporary nation's cultural patrimony are likely to evoke public and political support for preservation efforts more effectively than circumstances where the archaeological remains represent someone else, people and cultures supplanted by new people now in political control of the landscape, even if those new people embrace symbolically the sites marking the unfamiliar past and use many as prominent tourist attractions.

This latter situation applies in North America. Native American tribes and nations are descended from the cultures responsible for most archaeological sites formed before A.D. 1700. Looting does take place in sites associated with Euro-American and African American cultures, and artifacts from wells, cellars, cisterns, battle sites, and other contexts are subject to a brisk commercial market, but Native American sites and Native American artifacts are the focus of most trafficking and acknowledged looting in North America.

Mesoamerica and South America both have long histories of international antiquities trafficking and associated looting. Laws formulated to prohibit looting and the export of antiquities, some now many decades established, however imperfectly enforced, are evidence of official concern with site destruction and heritage loss. Information, mostly colloquial and qualitative, about looting associated with higher profile cultures, like the Maya and Moche, has been disseminated in many media.

Despite this general understanding that sites are looted and artifacts are disseminated to a global network of private collectors, corporate investors, and other recipients, most Americanists have not generally spent much time looking closely at the consequences of looting and merchandizing antiquities in their own backyard beyond the level of counting potholes in sites or bulldozer trenches through mounds. A few exceptions now in the literature, as well as the studies described in this volume, indicate that spending time studying the real impact on research in the Americas, particularly in North America, may be quite revealing.

Lithic artifacts are among the mundane workhorses of material culture studies for American prehistorians. Some types, especially those like Clovis and other Paleo-Indian specimens, and large, showy, early-to-middle Archaic types, are highly prized in the collector market. Although they do not command six figure prices, their desirability means occasional high sale prices that become common knowledge among the collecting fraternity. In his exceptional study of the world of modern flintknappers and the impact they have on collecting and on the raw material resource base, John C. Whittaker (2004) recounts the alleged sale of a dozen fake Clovis points for about $10,000 apiece in a transaction widely known as the Woody affair (Preston 1999; Whittaker 2004:253–260; Whittaker and Stafford 1999) as well as a subsequent reported sale at auction of a single Hemphill type point for $77,000.

At issue here is that Whittaker's careful and long-term study shows that there is a vast marketplace for both authentic old and modern lithics. Although many knappers claim they do not really want to sell points, or to have their points mistaken for old ones, carefully collected and quantified data indicate that, nearly a decade ago, modern flintknappers were likely turning out 1.5 million points a year (Whittaker 2004:266) and that huge quantities go to dealers and then to the commercial marketplace. Added to the take from an uncounted number of mundane sites that are literally placer-mined for stone tools, modern points disappear into a sea of stone tools moving in the commercial marketplace. Where do they go? How many end up in museum collections or are promoted as personally gathered private collections offered to archaeologists for study?

One million five hundred thousand dart points would require a mountain of raw stone each year. Flintknapper lore and practice target archaeologically well-known and knappable stone. One place to find such stone is in and around prehistoric quarries that are typically vast, unprotected, and sadly understudied site complexes. No substantial studies of quarry loss have been done, but modern flintknapping would seem to have an irrevocable impact on both the source and the end product of prehistoric lithic technology in North America.

The point here, so to speak, is not necessarily that we will soon be up to our knees in dart points, but that a careful examination of one class of objects, in this case beginning with the manufacture of modern examples, has yielded some significant revelations about the likely impact on the future study of lithic technologies and Paleo-Indian and Archaic tradition cultures in North America.

In the same vein, we now have available recently published compendia of fakery, trafficking, and the corruption of archaeological and art historical data sources for Mesoamerican and Andean South American cultures: *Faking the Ancient Andes* (Bruhns and Kelker 2010) and *Faking Ancient Mesoamerica* (Kelker and Bruhns 2010). Like Whittaker, the authors of these volumes undertake a thorough and careful look at faking and all its ramifications in one part of the Americas. While the point of entry into these twin studies is the history and character of fakery in two particular culture areas, the authors describe the scholarly and intellectual costs of fakes intermingled with archaeologically derived artifacts and looted antiquities in repositories that become the source of archaeological and historical research. The market in fakes has a further impact on site destruction. Whet the commercial market for, say, Mayan polychrome cylindrical jars, and the demand for more, looted or unknowingly forged, feeds the destruction.

The above-mentioned books indicate that the careful and revealing studies in this volume could be models for similar examinations in the Americas. If undertaken, we may find new ways to articulate the importance of site protection and the threat to intellectual inquiry by failing to diminish the looting menace.

References Cited

ABC News
2009 Heritage Win on Shipwreck Artefacts. ABC News [Australia], September 30.
Abu El-Haj, Nadia
2001 *Facts on the Ground: Archaeological Practice and Territorial Self-Fashioning in Israeli Society.* University of Chicago Press, Chicago.
Acar, Özgen
2001 Will "Blind Edip" Sing? *Archaeology* 54.1. http://www.archaeology.org/0101/newsbriefs/edip.html, accessed July 20, 2009.
Acar, Özgen, and Melik Kaylan
1988 The Hoard of the Century. *Connoisseur* 218:74–83.
Albright, William F.
1924 The Jordan Valley in the Bronze Age. *The Annual of the American Schools of Oriental Research* 6:13–74.
Ancient Coin Collectors Guild
2004–2009a Objectives. Electronic document, http://www.accg.us/about/objectives, accessed March 9, 2009.
2004–2009b Contributors. Electronic document, http://www.accg.us/about/contributor, accessed March 9, 2009.
2004–2009c Officers. Electronic document, http://www.accg.us/about/officers, accessed March 9, 2009.
2008 Dave Welsh Honored with ACCG Award. Electronic document, http://www.accg.us/issues/news/dave-welsh-honored-with-accg-award, accessed March 10, 2009.
Anderson, R. J., and A. Cahir
2003 *Surf Coast Wrecks.* Heritage Victoria, Melbourne.
ANSA
2007 Italian Archaeology Smugglers Uncovered. ANSA, January 31.

Antonova, Irina, Vladimir Tolstikov, and Mikhail Treister
  1996 *The Gold of Troy: Searching for Homer's Fabled City.* Thames and Hudson, London.
Appiah, Kwame Anthony
  2006 *Cosmopolitanism.* W. W. Norton, New York.
Azoulay, Ariella
  1994 With Open Doors: Museums and Historical Narratives in Israel's Public Space. In *Museum Culture, Histories, Discourses, Spectacles,* edited by Daniel J. Sherman and Irit Rogoff, pp. 85–109. University of Minnesota Press, Minneapolis.
Bachofen, Johann Jakob
  1861 *Mutterrecht und Urreligion.* Kröner, Leipzig.
Barbanera, Marcello
  1998 *L'archeologia degli italiani.* Editori Riuniti, Roma.
Barkat, Amiram
  2007 Collector Accused of Forging "James Ossuary" Says Old Photos Prove Authenticity. *Haaretz.com* February 9.
Bauman, Joel
  2004 Tourism, the Ideology of Design, and the Nationalized Past in Zippori/Sepphoris, an Israeli National Park. In *Marketing Heritage. Archaeology, and the Consumption of the Past,* edited by Yorke Rowan and Uzi Baram, pp. 205–228. AltaMira, Walnut Creek.
Beckmann, Martin
  1998 Numismatics and the Antiquities Trade. *Celator* 12(5):25–28.
Bennet, John
  1997 Homer and the Bronze Age. In *A New Companion to Homer,* edited by I. Morris and B. Powell, pp. 511–533. Brill, Leiden.
Betts, John
  1965 Notes on a Possible Minoan Forgery. *Annual of the British School at Athens* 60:203–206.
Bisheh, Ghazi
  2001 One Damn Illicit Excavation after Another: The Destruction of the Archaeological Heritage of Jordan. In *Trade in Illicit Antiquities: The Destruction of the World's Archaeological Heritage,* edited by Neil Brodie, Jenny Doole, and Colin Renfrew, pp. 115–118. McDonald Institute for Archaeological Research, Cambridge.
Blanck, Horst, and Giuseppe Proietti
  1986 *La Tomba dei Rilievi di Cerveteri.* Studi di archeologia, 1. Roma, De Luca.
Boardman, John
  2001 *The History of Greek Vases: Potters, Painters and Pictures.* Thames & Hudson, London.

2006 Archaeologists, Collectors, and Museums. In *Who Owns Objects? The Ethics and Politics of Collecting Cultural Artefacts*, edited by Eleanor Robson, Luke Treadwell, and Chris Gosden, pp. 33–46. Oxbow, Oxford.

Bolton, Glorney
1970 *Roman Century.* Viking Press, New York.

Bothmer, Dietrich von
1984 *A Greek and Roman Treasury.* The Metropolitan Museum of Art, New York.
1987 *Greek Vase Painting.* The Metropolitan Museum of Art, New York.

Bothmer, Dietrich von (editor)
1990 *Glories of the Past: Ancient Art from the Shelby White and Leon Levy Collection.* The Metropolitan Museum of Art, New York.

Bourdieu, Pierre
1984 *Distinction: A Social Critique of the Judgement of Taste.* Routledge, London.

Boylan, Patrick
1995 Illicit Trafficking in Antiquities and Museum Ethics. In *Antiquities: Trade or Betrayed*, edited by Kathryn W. Tubb, pp. 94–104. Archetype, London.

Bremer, Thomas S.
2009 The Brother of Jesus in Toronto. In *Resurrecting the Brother of Jesus: The James Ossuary Controversy and the Quest for Religious Relics*, edited by Ryan Byrne and Bernadette McNary-Zak, pp. 31–58. University of North Carolina Press, Chapel Hill.

Brodie, Neil
2006 Smoke and Mirrors. In *Who Owns Objects?* edited by Eleanor Robson, Luke Treadwell, and Chris Gosden, pp. 1–14. Oxbow, Oxford.
2010 Archaeological Looting and Economic Justice. In *Cultural Heritage Management, Policies and Issues in Global Perspective*, edited by Phyllis M. Messenger and George S. Smith, pp. 261–277. University Press of Florida, Gainesville.

Brodie, Neil, and Colin Renfrew
2005 Looting and the World's Archaeological Heritage: The Inadequate Response. *Annual Review of Anthropology* 34:343–428.

Broodbank, Cyprian
1992 The Spirit Is Willing. *Antiquity* 66:542–546.

Bruhns, Karen O., and Nancy L. Kelker
2010 *Faking the Ancient Andes.* Left Coast Press, Walnut Creek.

Burbules, Pete
1999a A New Source of Coins. Message posted to the Moneta-L list, June 8. Electronic document, http://groups.yahoo.com/group/Moneta-L/message/812, accessed March 10, 2009.
1999b RE: A New Source of Coins. Message posted to the Moneta-L list, June 8. Electronic document, http://groups.yahoo.com/group/Moneta-L/message/815, accessed March 10, 2009.

Burleigh, Nina
    2008   *Unholy Business: A True Tale of Faith, Greed, and Forgery in the Holy Land.* HarperCollins, New York.

Butcher, Kevin, and David W. J. Gill
    1990   Mischievous Pastime or Historical Science? *Antiquity* 64:946–950.
    1993   The Director, the Dealer, the Goddess, and Her Champions: The Acquisition of the Fitzwilliam Goddess. *American Journal of Archaeology* 97:383–401.

Byrne, Ryan, and Bernadette McNary-Zak (editors)
    2009   *Resurrecting the Brother of Jesus: The James Ossuary Controversy and the Quest for Religious Relics.* University of North Carolina Press, Chapel Hill.

Camp, John M.
    1986   *The Athenian Agora.* Thames and Hudson, New York.
    2008   *Who Owns Antiquity.* Princeton University Press, Princeton.

Canadian Museums Association
    1999   Ethical Guidelines. Canadian Museum Association. Electronic document, http://www.museums.ca/?n=15-293, accessed November 21, 2011.

Carradice, Ian (editor)
    1987   *Coinage and Administration in the Athenian and Persian Empires: The Ninth Oxford Symposium on Coinage and Monetary History.* BAR International Series 343. British Archaeological Reports, Oxford.

Cassidy, W.
    1991   Historic Shipwrecks and Blanket Declaration. *Bulletin of the Australasian Institute for Maritime Archaeology* 15(2):4–6.

Center for the Study of Democracy
    2007   Organized Crime in Bulgaria: Markets and Trends. Center for the Study of Democracy, Sofia. Electronic document, http://www.csd.bg/fileSrc.php?id=2394, accessed March 6, 2009.

Chavarria, Herbert R.
    2004   True Uncleaned Holyland Coins and Uncleaned Antoninianus and Much More. Message posted to Uncleaned Coins list, July 3. Electronic document, http://groups.yahoo.com/group/Uncleanedcoins/message/26037, accessed March 10, 2009.
    2006   RE: [NumisTreasures] Question for Dealers re. Low-End Coin Availability. Message posted to the Ancient Bulk Marketplace list, February 3. Electronic document, http://groups.yahoo.com/group/AncientBulkMarketplace/message/128, accessed March 10, 2009.

Chippindale, Christopher, and David W. J. Gill
    1993   Material and Intellectual Consequences of Esteem for Cycladic Figures. *American Journal of Archaeology* 97:601–659.
    2000   Material Consequences of Contemporary Classical Collecting. *American Journal of Archaeology* 104:463–511.

2001 Material Consequencies of Contemporary Classical Collecting. *American Journal of Archaaeology* 104:463–511.

Chippindale, Christopher, David W. J. Gill, Emily Salter, and Christian Hamilton
2001 Collecting the Classical World: First Steps in a Quantitative History. *International Journal of Cultural Property* 10:1–31.

Contreras, Daniel
2010 Huaqueros and Remote Sensing Imagery: Assessing Looting Damage in the Virú Valley, Peru. *Antiquity* 84:544–555.

Contreras, Daniel, and Neil Brodie
2010 Quantifying Destruction: An Evaluation of the Utility of Publicly-Available Satellite Imagery for Investigating Looting of Archaeological Sites in Jordan. *Journal of Field Archaeology* 35:101–104.

Cook, Robert M.
1989 The Francis-Vickers Chronology. *Journal of Hellenic Studies* 109:164–70.

Corbett, Peter E.
1960 The Burgon and Blacas Tombs. *Journal of Hellenic Studies* 80:52–60.

Coulomb, Jean
1979 Le "Prince aux Lis" de Knossos reconsideré. *Bulletin de Correspondance Hellenique* 103:29–50.
1990 Quartier sud de Knossos: Divinité ou athlète? *Cretan Studies* 2:99–110.

Cramer, Max
1999 *Treasures, Tragedies, and Triumphs of the Batavia Coast.* Scott Four Colour Print, Perth.

Cribb, J.
1994 Salvage Operation Turns into National Treasure. *The Australian* 30 March.

Cuno, James
2005 Museums, Antiquities, Cultural Property, and the US Legal Framework for Making Acquisitions. In *Who Owns the Past? Cultural Policy, Cultural Property, and the Law*, edited by K. Fitz Gibbon, pp. 143–157. Rutgers University Press / American Council for Cultural Policy, New Brunswick.
2008 *Who Owns Antiquity? Museums and the Battle over our Ancient Heritage.* Princeton University Press, Princeton.

Cuno, James (editor)
2004 *Whose Muse? Art Museums and the Public Trust.* Princeton University Press, Princeton.
2009 *Whose Culture?* Princeton University Press, Princeton.

Dayet, Maurice
1948 A Critical Study of the 'Ring of Nestor.' *Folklore* 59(2):88-90.

De Grummond, N.
1996 *An Encyclopedia of the History of Classical Archaeology.* Greenwood Press, Westport.

De Lachenal, L.
  1995 *Spolia*. Longanesi and C, Milan.
de Montebello, Philippe
  2007 Whose Culture Is It? Museums and the Collection of Antiquities. *The Berlin Journal* 15:33–37.
  2009 "And what do you propose should be done with those objects?". In *Whose Culture? The Promise of Museums and the Debate over Antiquities*, edited by J. Cuno, pp. 55–70. Princeton University Press, Princeton.
Dietrich, Reinhard
  2002 Cultural Property on the Move—Legally, Illegally. *International Journal of Cultural Property* 11(2):294–303.
Doumas, Christos
  1977 *Early Bronze Age Burial Habits in the Cyclades: Studies in Mediterranean Archaeology* 48. Goteborg, Paul Äströms.
Drew, T.
  2003 An Australian Shipwreck Collection with Provenance Recollected. Manuscript on file, Department of Archaeology, Flinders University, Adelaide.
Dyson, Stephen L.
  1998 *Ancient Marbles to American Shores*. University of Pennsylvania Press, Philadelphia.
  2006 *In Pursuit of Ancient Pasts*. Yale University Press, New Haven.
  2007 Review of Watson and Todeschini 2006. In *Journal of Hellenic Studies* 127:234–235.
Eakin, Hugh, and Elisabetta Povoledo
  2010 Italy Focuses on a Princeton Curator in an Antiquities Investigation. *New York Times* 3 June: C1.
Elia, Ricardo J.
  2001 Analysis of the Looting, Selling, and Collecting of Apulian Red-figure Vases: a Quantitative Approach. In *Trade in Illicit Antiquities: the Destruction of the World's Archaeological Heritage*, edited by Neil Brodie, Jenny Doole, and Colin Renfrew, pp. 145–153. McDonald Institute, Cambridge.
Elkins, Nathan T.
  2009 Coins, Contexts, and an Iconographic Approach for the 21st Century. In *Coins in Context I: New Perspectives for the Interpretation of Coin Finds*, edited by Hans-Markus von Kaenel and Fleur Kemmers, pp. 25–46. Studien zu Fundmünzen der Antike 23. Von Zabern, Mainz.
Ellis, A.
  2001 Toy Stories: Interpreting Childhood from the Victorian Archaeological Record. Unpublished honors thesis, Department of Archaeology, La Trobe University, Melbourne.

Evans, Arthur J.
  1896 Pillar and Tree-Worship in Mycenaean Greece. *Proceedings of the British Association* 45:934.
  1900 Knossos 1899. *Annual of the British School at Athens* [1899–1900]. 12–56.
  1901 Mycenaean Tree and Pillar Cult and Its Mediterranean Relations. *Journal of Hellenic Studies* 21:99–204.
  1921 *The Palace of Minos: A Comparative Account of the Successive Stages of the Early Cretan Civilization as Illustrated by the Discoveries at Knossos*, Vol. 1. Macmillan, London.
  1925 The "Ring of Nestor": A Glimpse into the Minoan After-World. *Journal of Hellenic Studies* 45:43–75.
  1928 *The Palace of Minos: A Comparative Account of the Successive Stages of the Early Cretan Civilization as Illustrated by the Discoveries at Knossos*, Vol. 2, Macmillan, London.
  1930 *The Palace of Minos: A Comparative Account of the Successive Stages of the Early Cretan Civilization as Illustrated by the Discoveries at Knossos*, Vol. 3. Macmillan, London.
  1935 *The Palace of Minos: A Comparative Account of the Successive Stages of the Early Cretan Civilization as Illustrated by the Discoveries at Knossos*, Vol. 4. Macmillan, London.
Exhibition Catalogue
  1990 *Euphronios, peintre à Athènes au VIe siècle avant J.-C.: Musée du Louvre, Paris, 18 septembre–31 décembre 1990*. Paris, Editions de la Réunion des musées nationaux.
Fielder, Wilfried
  1993 Art Robbery and the Protection of Cultural Property in Public International Law. In *Proceedings of the XIth International Numismatic Congress Organized for the 15th Anniversary of the Société Royale de Numismatique de Belgique, Brussels, September 8th–13th 1991,* edited by Tony Hackens and Ghislaine Moucharte, pp. 429–433. International Numismatic Commission, Louvain-la-Neuve.
Fielding, K. R.
  2003 A Pane in the Past: The *Loch Ard* Disaster and a Few Bits of Glass. *Bulletin of the Australasian Institute for Maritime Archaeology* 27:1–8.
Finley, Moses I.
  1975 *The Use and Abuse of History*. Viking Press, New York.
Fischer-Bossert, Wolfgang
  2008 *The Athenian Decadrachm*. Numismatic Notes and Monographs 168. American Numismatic Society, New York.
Flowers, G.
  2001 *Gilt Dragon:* Terrestrial Investigation. Skeleton and Coin Sites April, 2001. Report by the Maritime Archaeological Association of Western Australia, Perth.

Francis, E. David, and Michael Vickers
1981 Leagros kalos. *Proceedings of the Cambridge Philological Society* 207, n.s. 27:97–136.

Gatehouse, Jonathan
2005 Cashbox. *Maclean's* March 28:26–36.

Gesell, Geraldine
1985 *Town, Palace, and House Cult in Minoan Crete.* Studies in Mediterranean Archaeology, Vol. 67. P. Äströms förlag, Göteborg.

Gill, David W. J.
1990 Appendix. A One Mina Phiale from Kozani. *American Journal of Archaeology* 94:624–25.
1991 Pots and Trade: Spacefillers or *objets d'art. Journal of Hellenic Studies* 111:29–47.
1994 Positivism, Pots and Long-distance Trade. In *Classical Greece: Ancient Histories and Modern Archaeologies*, edited by Ian Morris, pp. 99–107. New Directions in Archaeology. Cambridge University Press, Cambridge.
1998 A Greek Price Inscription from Euesperides, Cyrenaica. *Libyan Studies* 29:83–88.
2003 Review of Nørskov 2002. In *Culture Without Context* 12:21–23.
2007a Review of Sotirakopoulou 2005. In *American Journal of Archaeology* 111:163–65.
2007b An Italian Cavalryman in Manhattan. Looting Matters Weblog, September 5. Electronic document, http://lootingmatters.blogspot.com/2007/09/italian-cavalryman-in-manhattan.html, accessed July 21, 2009.
2009a Looting Matters for Classical Antiquities: Contemporary Issues in Archaeological Ethics. *Present Pasts* 1:77–104.
2009b Exhibition review: Nostoi. December 2007, Palazzo del Quirinale, Rome. *The Journal of Art Crime* 1:70–71.
2009c Looting Matters: Why Are Ancient Coins from Cyprus Featured in a Suit against the US Department of State? *PR Newswire* June 26. http://www.prnewswire.com/cgi-bin/stories.pl?ACCT=109&STORY=/www/story/ 06-26-2009/0005051098&EDATE=, accessed July 21, 2009.
2010a Collecting Histories and the Market for Classical Antiquities. *Journal of Art Crime* 3:3–10.
2010b The Returns to Italy from North America: an Overview. *Journal of Art Crime* 3:105-09.

Gill, David W. J., and Christopher Chippindale
1993 Material and Intellectual Consequences of Esteem for Cycladic Figures. *American Journal of Archaeology* 97:601–659.
2002 The Trade in Looted Antiquities and the Return of Cultural Property: a British Parliamentary Inquiry. *International Journal of Cultural Property* 11:50–64.

2006   From Boston to Rome: Reflections on Returning Antiquities. *International Journal of Cultural Property* 13:311–331.

2007a   From Malibu to Rome: Further Developments on the Return of Antiquities. *International Journal of Cultural Property* 14:205–240.

2007b   The Illicit Antiquities Scandal: What it has Done to Classical Archaeology Collections. *American Journal of Archaeology* 111:571–574.

2008   South Italian Pottery in the Museum of Fine Arts, Boston Acquired Since 1983. *Journal of Field Archaeology* 33:462–472.

Gill, David W. J., and Michael Vickers

1995   They Were Expendable: Greek Vases in the Etruscan Tomb. *Revue des études anciennes* 97:225–49.

Göbl, Robert

1987   *Numismatik. Grundriß und wissenschaftliches System*. Battenberg, Munich.

Gordon, Beverly

1986   The Souvenir: Messenger of the Extraordinary. *Journal of Popular Culture* 20:135–146.

Gorecki, Joachim

1975   Studien zur Sitte der Münzbeigabe in römerzeitlichen Körpergräbern zwischen Rhein, Mosel und Somme. *Bericht der Römisch-Germanischen Kommission* 56:179–467.

Govies, Gordon

2002   Stunning New Evidence that Jesus Lived. Christianity Today. Electronic document http://www.christianitytoday.com/ct/2002/octoberweb-only/10-21-11.0.html, accessed November 21, 2011.

Green, J. N.

1977   *Australia's Oldest Wreck: The Historical Background and Archaeological Analysis of The Wreck of the English East India Company's Ship* Trial, *Lost off the Coast of Western Australia in 1622*. BAR Supplementary Series 27. British Archaeological Reports, Oxford.

1985   *Treasure from the* Vergulde Draeck. Western Australian Museum, Perth.

1986   The Survey and Identification of the English East India Company Ship Trial (1622). *The International Journal of Nautical Archaeology and Underwater Exploration* 15(3):195–204.

1989   The Loss of the Verenigde Oostindische Compagnie retourschip *Batavia*, Western Australia 1629. In *An Excavation Report and Catalogue of Artefacts*. BAR International Series 489. Archaeological Reports, Oxford.

1997   Trial. In *British Museum Encyclopaedia of Underwater and Maritime Archaeology*, edited by James P. Delgado, pp. 426. British Museum Press, London.

Griffiths, K.

1994   Shipwreck Amnesty Clangs to an End. *The* (Adelaide) *Advertiser* 2 April.

Hägg, R.
　1986　Die göttliche Epiphanie im minoischen Ritual. *Mitteilungen des Deutschen Archäologischen Instituts, Athenische Abteilung* 101:41–62.

Halbwachs, Maurice
　1992　*On Collective Memory*. University of Chicago Press, Chicago.

Hamilakis, Y., and E. Yalouri
　1999　Sacralising the Past. *Archaeological Dialogues* 6(2):115–135.

Harrington, Spencer P. M., William M. Calder III, David Demakopoulou, Katie Traill, Kenneth D. S. Capatin, Oliver Dickinson, and John G. Younger
　1999　Behind the Mask of Agamemnon. *Archaeology* 52(4):51–59.

Haselgrove, Colin, and David Wigg-Wolf (editors)
　2005　*Iron Age Coinage and Ritual Practices*. Studien zu Fundmünzen der Antike 20. Von Zabern, Mainz.

Haskell, F., and N. Penny
　1981　*Taste and the Antique*. Yale University Press, New Haven.

Heath, Dwight B.
　1973　Economic Aspects of Commercial Archaeology in Costa Rica. *American Antiquity* 38:259–265.

Henderson, G. H.
　1990　Twenty-Five Years of Maritime Archaeology in Australia. *Bulletin of the Australian Institute for Maritime Archaeology* 14(2):19–20.
　1997　Australia. In *British Museum Encyclopaedia of Underwater and Maritime Archaeology*, edited by James P. Delgado, pp. 44–45. British Museum Press, London.

Henderson, J. A.
　1993　*Phantoms of the Tryall*. St. Georges Books, Perth.

Heurgon, J.
　1989　Graffites étrusque au J. Paul Getty Museum. In *Greek Vases in the J. Paul Getty Museum* 4:181–86. J. Paul Getty Museum, Malibu.

Hibbert, C.
　1985　*Rome*. W. W. Norton, New York.
　1987　*The Grand Tour*. Methuen, London.

Hitchens, C.
　1987　*The Elgin Marbles: Should They Be Returned to Greece?* Verso, London.

Hobsbawm, Eric, and Terence Ranger (editors)
　1983　*The Invention of Tradition*. Cambridge University Press, New York.

Hollowell-Zimmer, Julie
　2003　Digging in the Dirt—Ethics and "Low-end" Looting. In *Ethical Issues in Archaeology*, edited by Larry J. Zimmerman, Karen D. Vitelli, and Julie Hollowell-Zimmer, pp. 45–56. AltaMira, Walnut Creek.

Hollowell, Julie
   2006a St. Lawrence Island's Legal Market in Archaeological Goods. In *Archaeology, Cultural Heritage, and the Antiquities Trade,* edited by Neil Brodie, Morag M. Kersel, Christina Luke, and Kathryn W. Tubb, pp. 98–132. University Press of Florida, Gainesville.
   2006b Moral Arguments on Subsistence Digging. In *The Ethics of Archaeology. Philosophical Perspectives on Archaeological Practice,* edited by Chris Scarre and Geoffrey Scarre, pp. 69–93. Cambridge University Press, Cambridge.

Hopkins, Clark
   1963 A Review of the Throne Room at Cnossos. *American Journal of Archaeology* 67:416–419.

Hopkins, Keith
   1980 Taxes and Trade in the Roman Empire (200 B.C.–A.D. 400). *Journal of Roman Studies* 70:101–125.

Hosty, Kieran
   1987 Historic Shipwreck Legislation and the Australian Diver: Past, Present, and Future. *Bulletin Australian Institute for Maritime Archaeology* 11(1):21–25.

Hosty, Kieran, and I. Stuart
   1994 Maritime Archaeology over the Last Twenty Years. *Australian Archaeology* 39:9–19.

Hoving, Thoms
   1993 *Making the Mummies Dance.* Simon and Schuster, New York.

Howgego, Christopher
   1995 *Ancient History from Coins.* Routledge, London and New York.

International Council of Museums (ICOM)
   1986 Code of Professional Ethics. ICOM, Paris.

Jacobovici, Simcha, and Felix Golubev
   2004 *James, Brother of Jesus: Holy Relic or Hoax? DVD Video.* Wellspring Media, New York.

Jeffery, W.
   1993 Maritime Archaeology: What's in It for Australians? *Bulletin Australian Institute for Maritime Archaeology* 17(2):1–6.
   1997 Australian Historic Shipwrecks Act. In *British Museum Encyclopaedia of Underwater and Maritime Archaeology,* edited by James P. Delgado, pp. 45–46. British Museum Press, London.

Jenkins, Ian, and Kim Sloan
   1996 *Vases and Volcanoes: Sir William Hamilton and his Collection.* British Museum Press, London.

Johnston, Alan W.
   2006 *Trademarks on Greek Vases: Addenda.* Aris and Phillips, Oxford.

Kalman, Matthew
    2009 The Burial Box of Jesus' Brother: Fraud? *Time*, September 5, 2009. http://www.time/com/time/world/article/0,8599,1920720,00.html.
Kelker, Nancy L., and Karen O. Bruhns
    2010 *Faking Ancient Mesoamerica*. Left Coast Press, Walnut Creek.
Kemmers, Fleur
    2006a *Coins for a Legion: An Analysis of the Coin Finds from the Augustan Legionary Fortress and Flavian Canabae Legionis at Nijmegen*. Studien zu Fundmünzen der Antike 21. Von Zabern, Mainz.
    2006b Coin Circulation in the Lower Rhine Area: Deliberate Policy or Laissez-Faire? In *Fontes Historiae: Studia in Honorem Demetrii Protase*, edited by Corneliu Gaiu and Cristian Găzdac, pp. 735–742. Editura Accent, Bistrița and Cluj-Napoca.
    2009 Sender or Receiver? Contexts of Coin Supply and Coin Use. In *Coins in Context I: New Perspectives for the Interpretation of Coin Finds*, edited by Hans-Markus von Kaenel and Fleur Kemmers, pp. 137–156. Studien zu Fundmünzen der Antike 23. Von Zabern, Mainz.
Kendall, F. J.
    1990 An Assessment of the Effectiveness of Existing Legislative Arrangements for Protecting and Preserving Australia's Underwater Cultural Heritage. Consultant's report to the Department of the Arts, Sport, the Environment, Tourism and Territories, Australia.
Kennedy, G. A.
    1998 *Discovery, Legislation, and Litigation*. Edited by J. N. Green, M. Stanbury, and F. Gaastra. The ANCODS Colloquium. Special Publication No. 3, Australian National Centre of Excellence for Maritime Archaeology. Western Australian Maritime Museum, Fremantle.
Kersel, Morag M.
    2006 Licensed to Sell: The Legal Trade of Antiquities in Israel. Unpublished Ph.D. dissertation, Department of Archaeology, University of Cambridge, Cambridge.
Killen, J. T.
    2001 Religion at Pylos: The Evidence of the Fn Tablets. *Aegaeum* 22:435–443.
Knapp, Stephen
    1999 A New Source of Coins. Message posted to the Moneta-L list, June 8. Electronic document, http://groups.yahoo.com/group/Moneta-L/message/822, accessed March 10, 2009.
Knott, P.
    2001 Tokens of a Tragedy. *Signals* 54:24–25.
Koening, Franz E.
    1999 Les monnaies. In *La nécropole gallo-romaine d'Avenches "En Chaplix". Fouilles 1987–1992, 2. Étude du mobilier. Aventicum X*, edited by Daniel

Castella, Chantal Martin Pruvot, Heidi Amrein, Anike Duvanchelle, and Franz E. Koenig, pp. 427–462. Cahiers d'Archéologies Romande 78. Lausanne.

Kraay, Colin M.
1976 *Archaic and Classical Greek Coins*. University of California Press, Los Angeles and Berkeley.

Krmnicek, Stefan
2009 Das Konzept der Objektbiographie in der antiken Numismatik. In *Coins in Context I: New Perspectives for the Interpretation of Coin Finds*, edited by Hans-Markus von Kaenel and Fleur Kemmers, pp. 47–59. Studien zu Fundmünzen der Antike 23. Von Zabern, Mainz.

Kurtz, Donna C. (editor)
1989 *Greek Vases: Lectures by J.D. Beazley*. Clarendon Press, Oxford.

Lange, Frederick W.
1976 Costa Rica and the "Subsistence Archaeologist." *Current Anthropology* 17:305–307.

Lapatin, Kenneth
2002 *Mysteries of the Snake Goddess: Art, Desire, and the Forging of History*. Houghton Mifflin, New York.

Lapp, Paul W.
1966 The Cemetery at Bab edh-Dhra', Jordan. *Archaeology* 19(2):104–111.

Latour, Bruno
1993 *We Have Never Been Modern*. Harvester Wheatsheaf, New York.

Lattimore, Richard A. (editor and translator)
1961 *The Iliad of Homer*. University of Chicago Press, Chicago.

Lemaire, André
2002 Burial Box of James, Brother of Jesus. *Biblical Archaeology Review* 28(6):24–33, 70.

Lissarrague, François
1990 *The Aesthetics of the Greek Banquet: Images of Wine and Ritual*. Princeton University Press. Princeton.

Loney, J.
1981 *An Atlas History of Australian Shipwrecks*. A. H. and A. W. Reed, Sydney.

McCane, Byron
2009 Archaeological Context and Controversy. In *Resurrecting the Brother of Jesus: The James Ossuary Controversy and the Quest for Religious Relics*, edited by Ryan Byrne and Bernadette McNary-Zak, pp. 19–30. University of North Carolina Press, Chapel Hill.

McCarthy, M.
2006 The Dutch on Australian Shores: The *Zuytdorp* Tragedy—Unfinished Business. In *Dutch Connection, 400 Years of Australian-Dutch Maritime Links, 1606–2006*, pp. 94–109. Australian National Maritime Museum.

McCreery, David W.
　1996　A Salvage Operation at Bāb adh-Dhrā. *Annual of the Department of Antiquities of Jordan* 40:51–62.

McDonald, William
　1990　*Progress into the Past: The Rediscovery of Mycenaean Civilization.* Indiana University Press, Bloomington.

MacEnroe, John
　1995　Sir Arthur Evans and Edwardian Archaeology. *Classical Bulletin* 71:36–57.

MacGillivray, Joseph A.
　2000　*Minotaur: Sir Arthur Evans and the Archaeology of the Minoan Myth.* Hill and Wang, New York.

MacGillivray, Joseph A., J. M. Driessen, and L. H. Sackett
　2000　*The Palaikastro Kouros: A Minoan Chryselephantine Statuette and Its Aegean Bronze Age Context.* British School at Athens Studies 6. Athens.

McKinnon, R. J.
　1991　The Kangaroo Island Shipwreck Survey and Community Involvement. *Bulletin of the Australian Institute for Maritime Archaeology* 15(2):37–40.

McPhee, E.
　2004　An Analysis of Chinese Cash Coins from the Wreck of the *SS Mecca*, 1878. Unpublished honors thesis, Department of Archaeology, James Cook University, Townsville, Australia.

Maggio, M.
　1998　A Change of Climate. *The Art Newspaper* 86(November):45.

Magness, Jodi
　2005　Ossuaries and the Burials of Jesus and James. *Journal of Biblical Literature* 124:121–154.

Manacorda, D., and R. Tamassia
　1985　*Il piccone del regime.* Armando Curcio, Roma Editore.

Marchand, Suzanne L.
　1996　*Down from Olympus* Princeton University Press, Princeton, NJ.

Marinatos, Nanno
　1993　*Minoan Religion. Ritual, Image, and Symbol.* University of South Carolina Press, Columbia.

Martin, Christopher
　1996　*Ancient Art: The Grand Tour.*

Matsuda, David
　1998　The Ethics of Archaeology, Subsistence Digging, and Artifact Looting in Latin America: Point, Muted Counterpoint. *International Journal of Cultural Property* 7:87–97.
　2005　Subsistence diggers. In *Who Owns the Past? Cultural Policy, Cultural Property, and the Law,* edited by Kate Fitz Gibbon, pp. 255–268, Rutgers University Press, New Brunswick.

Matthews, Roy, and DeWitt Platt
 2009 *The Western Humanities*. McGraw Hill, New York.
Mead, Rebecca
 2007 Den of Antiquity: The Met and the Antiquities Market. *The New Yorker* 9 April:52–61.
Media Release
 1993 Senator Bob McMullan, The Search is on for Australia's Lost Shipwrecks. Press release, Department of the Arts and Administrative Services, April 30, Canberra.
Meyer, K. E.
 1973 *The Plundered Past*. Athenaeum, New York.
Miles, M.
 2008 *Art as Plunder*. Cambridge University Press, Cambridge.
Miller, Stephen G.
 2004 *Ancient Greek Athletics*. Yale University Press, New Haven and London.
Momigliano, Arnaldo
 1950 Ancient History and the Antiquarian. *Journal of the Warburg and Courtald Institute*s 13(3/4):285–315.
Mommsen, Theodor
 1895 In Proceedings of the Numismatic Society. *Numismatic Chronicle* 15:20–21.
Moon, Warren G., and Louise Berge
 1979 *Greek Vase-painting in Midwestern Collections*. Chicago, Art Institute of Chicago.
Moreland, Milton
 2009 Christian Artifacts in Documentary Film. The Case of the James Ossuary. In *Resurrecting the Brother of Jesus: The James Ossuary Controversy and the Quest for Religious Relics*, edited by Ryan Byrne and Bernadette McNary-Zak, pp. 73–136. University of North Carolina Press, Chapel Hill.
Murphy, Fiona
 1996 Sale of the Centuries. (London) *Guardian* 2 November.
Muscarella, Oscar White
 2000 *The Lie Became Great: The Forgery of Ancient Near Eastern Cultures*. Styx, Groningen.
 2009 The Fifth Column within the Archaeological Realm: The Great Divide. Saving Antiquities for Everyone (SAFE). Electronic document, http://www.savingantiquities.org/pdf/OM5thcolumn.pdf
Newnham, David
 1996 Storm in a Dipper Cup. (London) *Guardian* 7 December.

Niemeier, W.-D.

1987 Das Stuckrelief des Prinzen mit der Federkrone aus Knossos und minoische Götterdarstellungen. *Mitteilungen des Deutschen Archäologischen Instituts, Athenische Abteilung* 102:65–98.

1988 The Priest-King Fresco from Knossos: A New Reconstruction and Interpretation. In *Problems in Greek Prehistory: Papers Presented at the Centenary Conference of the British School of Archaeology at Athens, Manchester, April 1986*, edited by E. B. French and K. A. Wardle, pp. 235–244. Bristol.

Nilsson, Martin

1949 *The Minoan-Mycenaean Religion and Its Survival in Greek Religion*. 2nd ed. Biblio and Tannen, New York.

Nutley, D.

2006 The *Queen of Nations*: A Shipwreck with Influence. In *Underwater Cultural Heritage at Risk, Special Edition,* pp. 11–13. ICOMOS, Munich.

O'Keefe, Patrick J.

1997 Trade in Antiquities. *Reducing Destruction and Theft*. Archetype, London.

Osborne, Robin G.

1996 Pots, Trade and the Archaic Greek Economy. *Antiquity* 70:31–44.

2001 Why did Athenian Pots Appeal to the Etruscans? *World Archaeology* 33:277–295.

Özgen, Ilknur, and Jean Öztürk

1996 *The Lydian Treasure: Heritage Recovered*. Istanbul, Republic of Turkey, Ministry of Culture General Directorate of Monuments and Museums.

Padgett, J. Michael

2001 Ajax and Achilles on a Calyx-krater by Euphronios. *Record of the Art Museum, Princeton University* 60:3–17.

Panagiotaki, Marina

1993 The Temple Repositories of Knossos: Evans's Notes. *Annual of the British School at Athens* 88:49–91.

Parcak, Sarah

2009 *Satellite Remote Sensing for Archaeology*. Routledge, London.

Peachey, K.

2002 Assessment of the Threat Posed to Unrecovered Silver Coins on the *Zuytdorp* (Located on the Western Australian Coast) by Acts of Theft. Confidential report of the Strategic Intelligence Team, Australian Federal Police, Western Operations.

Persson, Axel W.

1942 *The Religion of Greece in Prehistoric Times*. University of California Press, Berkeley.

Peter, Markus

2001 *Untersuchungen zu den Fundmünzen aus Augst und Kaiseraugst*. Studien zu Fundmünzen der Antike 17. Gebhart Mann, Berlin.

Philippou, C.
    2004   Collection Management for Shipwreck Relics: Amnesty Significance Assessment Victoria 2003 Interim Report. *Bulletin of the Australasian Institute for Maritime Archaeology* 28:25–32.

Picón, Carlos A., Joan R. Mertens, Elizabeth J. Milleker, Christopher S. Lightfoot, and Seán Hemingway
    2007   *Art of the Classical World in the Metropolitan Museum of Art: Greece, Cyprus, Etruria, Rome*. The Metropolitan Museum of Art, New York.

Pini, Ingo
    1998   The "Ring of Nestor." *Oxford Journal of Archaeology* 17:1–12.

Politis, Konstantinos D.
    2002   Dealing with the Dealers and Tomb Robbers: The Realities of the Archaeology of the Ghor es-Safi in Jordan. In *Illicit Antiquities: The Theft of Culture and the Extinction of Archaeology*, edited by Neil Brodie and Kathryn W. Tubb, pp. 257–267. Routledge, London.

Pollock, Susan
    2008   Archaeology as a Means for Peace or a Source of Violence? An Introduction. *Archaeologies: Journal of the World Archaeological Congress* 4(3):356–367.

Potts, A.
    1994   *Flesh and the Ideal*. Yale University Press, New Haven.

Preston, Douglas
    1999   Woody's Dream. *New Yorker* 75(34):80–87.

Rehak, Paul
    1997   The Role of Religious Painting in the Function of the Minoan Villa: The Case of Ayia Triadha. In *The Function of the Minoan Villa*, edited by R. Hagg, pp. 163–174. Skrifter utgivna av Svenska Institutet Athen 40. Stockholm.

Reich, John, and Lawrence Cunningham
    2009   *Culture and Values: A Survey of the Humanities*. Cengage, New York.

Renfrew, Colin
    1985   *Archaeology of Cult: The Sanctuary at Phylakop*. Thames and Hudson, London.

Ridgway, Brunilde Sismondo
    2007   Review of Picón et al. 2007. In *Bryn Mawr Classical Review*. Available at http://ccat.sas.upenn.edu/bmcr/2007/2007-08-10.html (accessed on May 1, 2008).

Robinson, Walter V.
    1998   Claims to Greek Goddesses. *The Boston Globe* 4 April.

Robson, F.
    1994   Treasures of the Deep. *Good Weekend* 15 January:16–21.

Rodrigues, J. A.
    2009a   An Amnesty Assessed: Human Impact on Shipwreck Sites: The Australian Case. *The International Journal of Nautical Archaeology* 38(1):153–162.

2009b Evidence in the Private Sphere: Assessing the Practicality of Amnesties to Record Lost Information. *Archaeologies: Journal of the World Archaeological Congress* 5(1):92–108.

2009c Property Search and Seizing of Relics by Commonwealth Investigators Allegedly Recovered from the "Batavia" (1629) Shipwreck Site between 10–13 April 2009. Special publication, No. 248. Confidential report of the Department of Maritime Archaeology, Western Australian Museum.

2010 Managing Australia's Private Shipwreck Collections from Early Souvenir Hunting Activities. In *World Universities Congress, 20/24 October, Çanakkale, Turkey, Proceedings II*, pp. 1563–1570. Çanakkale Onsekiz Mart University, Çanakkale.

2011 Finders Keepers: An Examination of the Impact of Diver Interaction with Shipwrecks as Revealed by the 1993 Amnesty Collections. Unpublished Ph.D. thesis, Archaeology, School of Social and Cultural Studies, University of Western Australia, Perth.

Rollston, Christopher, and Andrew G. Vaughn

2005 Epilogue: Methodological Musings from the Field. *SBL Forum*. http://sblsite.org/Article.aspx?ArticleID-376.

Rose, Jerome C., and Dolores L. Burke

2004 Making Money from Buried Treasure. *Culture without Context* 14:4–8.

Rose, Mark, and Özgen Acar

1995 Turkey's War on the Illicit Antiquities Trade. *Archaeology* March/April:45–56.

Rouet, Philippe

2001 *Approaches to the Study of Attic Vases: Beazley and Pottier*. Oxford Monographs on Classical Archaeology. Oxford University Press, Oxford.

Royal Ontario Museum

2001 Board Policy: Ethics and Conduct. Available at http://www.rom.on.ca/about/pdf/boardpolicies/ethicsconduct.pdf. Accessed November 21, 2011.

2002a ROM to display James Ossuary. 1st Century C.E. Press release, Royal Ontario Museum, October 25.

2002b The James Ossuary Will Open on November 15 at 4pm. Press release, Royal Ontario Museum, November 7.

2002c Media Preview for the James Ossuary. Press release, Royal Ontario Museum, November 12.

2003 Royal Ontario Museum Statement: Oded Golan's arrest/James Ossuary. Press release, Royal Ontario Museum, July 23.

Russmann, Edna

2009 *Unearthing the Truth: Egypt's Pagan and Coptic Sculpture*. Brooklyn Museum, Brooklyn.

Rutkowski, Bogdan

1986 *The Cult Places of the Aegean*. Yale University Press, New Haven.

1991 *Petsophas: A Cretan Peak Sanctuary.* Warsaw.
Sakellarakis, J.
  1973 Über die Echtheit des sogenannten Nestorringes. Πεπραγμένα του Ι' Κρητολογικου Συνεδρίου, Α' 303–318.
  1994 Το δακττυλίδι του Νέστορα: Είναι γυήσιο? In Λοίβη εις μνήμην Ανδρέα Γ'. Καλοκαιρινού. Εταιρεία Κρητικών Σπουδών [Iraklion] 93–106.
Sakellarakis and E. Sapouna-Sakellarakis
  1981 Drama of Death in a Minoan Temple. *National Geographic* 159(2): 205–222.
Sayles, Wayne
  2004 Through the Looking Glass: Hijacked by Zealots. *Celator* 18(8). http://www.accg.us/issues/editorials/pro/zealots.
  2005 Archaeology: A Wolf in Sheep's Clothing? ACCG Editorial, January 1. Electronic document, http://www.accg.us/issues/editorials/pro/wolf, accessed March 6, 2009.
  2007a Intrinsic Interests. Coin Link. Electronic document, http://www.coinlink.com/News/ancients/intrinsic-interests, accessed March 10, 2009.
  2007b Yes, It's a War. Ancient Coin Collecting Weblog, July 13. Electronic document, http://ancientcoincollecting.blogspot.com/2007/07/yes-its-war.html, accessed July 21, 2009.
  2008 Registration. *Celator* 22(11):45.
Sayre, Henry
  2009 *Discovering the Humanities.* Pierson Higher Education, Saddle River.
Scham, Sandra
  2009 Diplomacy and Desired Pasts. *Journal of Social Archaeology* 9(2):163–199.
Schaub, R. Thomas
  2008 Cultural Artifacts of the EB I Tombs. In *The Early Bronze Age I Tombs and Burials of Bab edh-Dhra', Jordan,* edited by Donald J. Ortner and Bruno Frohlich, pp. 25–44. AltaMira, Lanham.
Schaub, R. Thomas, and Walter E. Rast
  1989 *Bab edh-Dhra: Excavations in the Cemetery Directed by Paul W. Lapp (1965–67).* Eisenbrauns, Winona Lake.
Settis, S.
  1999 *Laocoonte Donizelli Editore.* Roma.
Sgubini, Anna Maria Moretti
  1999 *Euphronios epoiesen: un dono d'eccezione ad Ercole Cerite.* Rome, L'Erma di Bretschneider.
Shanks, Hershel
  2005 Update. Finds or Fakes? *Biblical Archaeology Review* 31(2):58–69.
  2009 Hershel Shanks: "Prosecutorial Misconduct" in Israeli Forgery Case? *Biblical Archaeology Review.* http://www.bib-arch.org/debates/antiquities-trial-06.asp.

Shanks, Hershel and Ben Witherington III
　2003　*The Brother of Jesus: The Dramatic Story and Meaning of the First Archaeological Link to Jesus and his Family.* HarperCollins, New York.

Shavit, Yaakov
　1997　Archaeology, Political Culture, and Culture in Israel. In *The Archaeology of Israel: Constructing the Past, Interpreting the Present,* Vol. 237, edited by Neil A. Silberman and David Small, pp. 48–61. *Journal for the Study of the Old Testament* Supplement Series. Sheffield Academic Press, Sheffield.

Sheedy, K. A., and Ch. Papageorgiadou-Banis (editors)
　1997　*Numismatic Archaeology, Archaeological Numismatics. Proceedings of an International Conference Held to Honour Dr. Mando Oeconomides in Athens 1995.* Oxbow Monograph 75. Australian Institute at Athens, Oxford.

Shelmerdine, Cynthia (editor)
　2008　*The Cambridge Companion to the Aegean Bronze Age.* Cambridge University Press, New York.

Silberman, Neil
　1997　Structuring the Past: Israelis, Palestinians, and the Symbolic Authority of Archaeological Monuments." In *The Archaeology of Israel: Constructing the Past, Interpreting the Present,* edited by Neil A. Silberman and David Small, pp. 62–81. Sheffield University Press, Sheffield.

Silver, Vernon
　2009　*The Lost Chalice: the Epic Hunt for a Priceless Masterpiece.* William Morrow, New York.

Slayman, Andrew L.
　1998　The Case of the Golden Phiale. *Archaeology* May/June:36–49.
　2006　The Trial in Rome. *Archaeology On-line* February 6. http://www.archaeology.org/online/features/italytrial/, accessed November 10, 2009.

Smith, T.
　1992　The *Queen of Nations:* One Hundred and Twelve Years On. *Bulletin of the Australian Institute for Maritime Archaeology* 16(2):9–16.

Snible, Ed
　2008　Guest Editorial. *Celator* 22(10):2, 4.

Snodgrass, Anthony M.
　1998　*Homer and the Artists: Text and Picture in Early Greek Art.* Cambridge University Press, Cambridge.

Sofia News Agency
　2008　Bulgaria Police Bust 19-Member Group of Treasure-Hunters. *Sofia News Agency* February 5. http://www.novinite.com/view_news.php?id=90081, accessed March 6, 2009.

Southgate, T.
　1993　Call to Declare Old Ship Relics. *South Western Times* 27 May.

Sotirakopoulou, Peggy
   2005 *The "Keros Hoard": Myth or Reality? Searching for the Lost Pieces of a Puzzle.* Athens, N.P. Goulandris Foundation - Museum of Cycladic Art.

Sox, D.
   1987 *Unmasking the Forger: The Dossena Deception.* Universe Books, New York.

Spanel, Donald
   2001 Two Groups of "Coptic" Sculpture and Relief in the Brooklyn Museum of Art. *Journal of the American Research Center in Egypt* 38:89–113.

Staley, David P.
   1993 St. Lawrence Island's Subsistence Diggers: A New Perspective on Human Effects on Archaeological Sites. *Journal of Field Archaeology* 20:347–355.

St. Clair, William
   1998 *Lord Elgin and the Marbles.* Oxford University Press, Oxford.

Stirling, L.
   2005 *The Learned Collector.* University of Michigan Press, Ann Arbor.

Tillyard, E. M. W.
   1923 *The Hope Vases: a Catalogue and a Discussion of the Hope Collection of Greek Vases with an Introduction on the History of the Collection and on Late Attic and South Italian Vases.* Cambridge University Press, Cambridge.

Tokeley, Jonathan
   2006 *Rescuing the Past.* Imprint Academic, Exeter.

Tompkins, J. F. (editor)
   1983 *Wealth of the Ancient World: the Nelson Bunker Hunt and William Herbert Hunt Collections.* Fort Worth (TX), Kimbell Art Museum.

Tubb, Kathryn W., and Neil Brodie
   2001 From Museum to Mantelpiece: The Antiquities Trade in the United Kingdom. In *Destruction and Conservation of Cultural Property,* edited by Robert Layton, Peter G. Stone, and Julian Thomas, pp. 102–116. Routledge, London.

van Velzen, Diura T.
   1996 The World of Tuscan Tomb Robbers: Living with the Local Community and the Ancestors. *International Journal of Cultural Property* 5:111–126.

Vickers, Michael, and David Gill
   1994 *Artful Crafts: Ancient Greek Silverware and Pottery.* Clarendon Press, Oxford.

Vikan, Gary
   1981 *Questions of Authenticity among the Arts of Byzantium: Catalogue of an Exhibition Held at Dumbarton Oaks, January 7–May 11, 1981.* Dumbarton Oaks, Washington, D.C.

Volpe, L. D.
   2009 *L'Arma per l'Arte: Antologia di meraviglie.* Sillabe, Rome.

von Kaenel, Hans-Markus
　1994　Die antike Numismatik und ihr Material. *Schweizer Münzblätter* 44(173):1–12.
　1995　La numismatica antica e il suo material. *Bollettino di Numismatica* 13(1):213–223.
　1999　Zum Münzumlauf im augusteischen Rom anhand der Funde aus dem Tiber – mit einem Nachtrag zur geldgeschichtlichen Bedeutung der Münzfunde in Kalkrise. In *Rom, Germanien, und die Ausgrabungen von Kalkriese. Internationaler Kongress der Universität Osnabrück und des Landschaftsverbandes Osnabrücker Land e.V. vom 2 bis 5 September 1996*, edited by Wolfgang Schlüter and Rainer Wiegels, pp. 363–379. Osnabrücker Forschungen zu Altertum und Antike Rezeption 1. Osnabrück.
　2009　Coins in Context—A Personal Approach. In *Coins in Context I: New Perspectives for the Interpretation of Coin Finds*, edited by Hans-Markus von Kaenel and Fleur Kemmers, pp. 9–24. Studien zu Fundmünzen der Antike 23. Von Zabern, Mainz.
von Kaenel, Hans-Markus, and Fleur Kemmers (editors)
　2009　*Coins in Context I: New Perspectives for the Interpretation of Coin Finds*. Studien zu Fundmünzen der Antike 23. Von Zabern, Mainz.
Walker, Alan S.
　1977　The Coin Market versus the Numismatist, Archaeologist, and Art Historian. *Journal of Field Archaeology* 4:255–258.
Wall, S. J. H. Musgrave, and P. Warren
　1986　Human Bones from a Late Minoan I B House at Knossos. *Annual of the British School at Athens* 81:333–338.
Warren, Peter
　1987　The Ring of Minos. EI_A_INH [Iraklion], 485–500.
　1988　*Minoan Religion as Ritual Action: Studies in Mediterranean Archaeology and Literature, Pocket Book 72.* A_stro_ms Fo_rlag, Gothenburg.
　1990　Of Baetyls. *Opuscula Atheniensia* 18:193–206.
Wartenberg Kagan, Ute
　2007　From the Executive Director. *American Numismatic Society Magazine* 6(1):7.
Watson, Peter
　1997　*Sotheby's: The Inside Story*. Random House, New York.
Watson, Peter
　2002　The Investigation of Frederick Schultz. *Culture without Context* 10:21–26.
Watson, Peter, and Cecilia Todeschini
　2006　*The Medici Conspiracy: the Illicit Journey of Looted Antiquities from Italy's Tomb Raiders to the World's Great Museums*. Public Affairs, New York.
　2007　*The Medici Conspiracy*. PublicAffairs, New York.

Waxman S.
  2008 *Loot*. Henry Holt, New York.
Weiss, R.
  1969 *The Renaissance Discovery of Classical Antiquity*. Basil Blackwell, Oxford.
Welsh, David
  2004 Uncle Wayne Wants YOU. Message posted to Moneta-L list, August 5. Electronic document, http://groups.yahoo.com/group/Moneta-L/message/62475, accessed March 9, 2009.
  2007 ***ALERT Cyprus Restriction on Coins Went Through***. Message posted to Moneta-L list, July 15. Electronic document, http://groups.yahoo.com/group/Moneta-L/message/84399, accessed March 9, 2009.
Westbrook, Kent C., and J. A. McEntire III
  1982 *Legacy in Clay: Prehistoric Ceramic Art of Arkansas*. Rose Publishing Company, Little Rock.
Wharton, Annabel Jane
  2006 *Selling Jerusalem: Relics, Replicas, Theme Parks*. University of Chicago Press, Chicago.
Whittaker, John C.
  2004 *American Flintknappers*. University of Texas Press, Austin.
Whittaker, John C., and Michael Stafford
  1999 Replicas, Fakes, and Art: The Twentieth Century Stone Age and Its Effects on Archaeology. *American Antiquity* 64(2):203–214.
Wigg-Wolf, David
  2009 Sites as Context. In *Coins in Context I: New Perspectives for the Interpretation of Coin Finds*, edited by Hans-Markus von Kaenel and Fleur Kemmers, pp. 109–125. Studien zu Fundmünzen der Antike 23. Von Zabern, Mainz.
Wilford, John Noble
  2002 Jesus Inscription on Stone May Be Earliest Ever Found. *New York Times*, October 22, 2002. www.nytimes.com/2002/10/22/science/22JESU.html.
Williams, Dyfri
  1991 Onesimos and the Getty Iliupersis. In *Greek vases in the J. Paul Getty Museum* 5, edited by M. True:41–64. Occasional Papers on Antiquities 7. J. Paul Getty Museum, Malibu.
  1992 The Brygos Tomb Reassembled and 19th-century Commerce in Capuan Antiquities. *American Journal of Archaeology* 96:617–636.
Winckelmann, J. J.
  2006 *History of the Art of Antiquity*. Getty Publications, Los Angeles.
Witschonke, Rick
  2009 Guest Editorial. *Celator* 23(1):4, 22.
Woodford, J.
  1993 Diver Gets Some Treasure off His Chest. *Sydney Morning Herald* 15 October.

Wright, James
    1995   Review of *Nanno Marinatos, Minoan Religion. Ritual, Image, and Symbol.* *Bryn Mawr Classical Review* 95(3):17.
    2004   The Mycenaean Feast. Hesperia 73.2. The American School of Classical Studies at Athens, Princeton.

Yalouri, E.
    2001   *The Acropolis.* Oxford, Berg.

Younger, John
    1976   Bronze Age Representations of Aegean Bull-Leaping. *American Journal of Archaeology* 80:125–137.
    1983   A New Look at Aegean Bull-Leaping. *Muse* 17:72–80.
    1995   Bronze Age Representations of Aegean Bull-Games, III. *Aegaeum* 12:507–545.

Zerubavel, Yael
    1995   *Recovered Roots: Collective Memory and the Making of Israeli National Traditions.* University of Chicago Press, Chicago.

About the Contributors

ALEX W. BARKER is Director of the Museum of Art and Archaeology at the University of Missouri. He has chaired the ethics committees of both the Society for American Archaeology and the American Anthropological Association, as well as serving on the AAM Cultural Property Task Force that developed stricter guidelines for the ethical acquisition of antiquities by American museums.

NEIL BRODIE is a Senior Research Fellow at the Scottish Centre for Crime and Justice Research, based at the University of Glasgow. He was previously a Research Fellow at Stanford University's Archaeology Center, and Research Director of the Illicit Antiquities Research Centre at the University of Cambridge.

DANIEL CONTRERAS employs a variety of digital methods in his archaeological fieldwork in Peru, Jordan, and Mexico. He is currently pursuing his interests in geoarchaeological approaches to long-term human-environment interactions as a Humboldt Postdoctoral Fellow at Kiel University.

STEPHEN L. DYSON is Park Professor of Classics at the University of Buffalo. He has written extensively on the History of Archaeology and the History of Collecting in Europe and the United States. His most recent work is The Pursuit of Ancient Pasts (New Haven 2006).

About the Contributors

ANN M. EARLY is State Archeologist, Arkansas Archeological Survey, and Associate Professor, Anthropology, University of Arkansas.

NATHAN T. ELKINS is Assistant Professor of Art History, Greek and Roman Art, at Baylor University. He is a specialist in Roman coins and Roman iconography and has worked as a numismatist for excavations in Israel.

SENTA GERMAN is Associate professor of Classics and General Humanities and Art and Design at Montclair State University. Her area of research is the Aegean Bronze Age; she is currently working on a book about Minoan and Mycenaean women.

DAVID GILL is Professor of Archaeological Heritage and Head of the Division of Humanities, University Campus Suffolk.

MORAG M. KERSEL is an Assistant Professor in the Department of Anthropology at DePaul University. Her research investigates the efficacy of law in archaeological site protection. She currently co-directs the Galilee Prehistory Project, investigating the Chalcolithic of northern Israel and the Follow the Pots project, tracking the movement of Early Bronze Age pots from mortuary landscapes in Jordan to the global antiquities market.

PAULA KAY LAZRUS is an Assistant Professor in the Institute for Core Studies at St. John's University. She is a member of the Bova Marina Archaeological Project, and former chairperson of the SAA's Committee on Ethics.

DR. JENNIFER RODRIGUES is currently the Collections Manager at the Western Australian Museum's Department of Maritime Archaeology in Fremantle. In the past, Jennifer has worked as a researcher at the Mary Rose Museum (UK), as a consultant across Australia, as well as a lecturer in the Maritime Archaeology postgraduate programme at Flinders University in Adelaide.

Index

Acropolis, 49
Aegean Bronze Age. *See* Bronze Age, Aegean
Agamemnon, 65
American Numismatic Society (ANS), 102, 106
Amnesty, 83–88
Ancient Coin Collectors Guild (ACCG), 100–101, 102–4
ancient coins: central to illicit antiquities trade, 91, 106; corpora of, 96; hoards of, 96; ideology on, 95; importance of context in study of, 95–96; as important part of the archaeological record, 95; lobbying by dealers for unrestricted trade in, 100–104; as major small finds at Greek and Roman sites, 93; most contribute little to numismatic science, 96; organization of trade in, 97–99; role of collectors in reducing looting of, 104–106, 107; unethical side of trade in, 92
Anemospilia, Crete, 66
an-Naq', Jordan, 21, 22
antiquities trade: coin dealers lobby for unrestricted, 100–104; deceptions of scholars and public by, 128–29; rise of, 51–53; statements of provenience used by dealers to increase historical interest in, 21–22
Appiah, Kwame, 35, 54
Apulian pottery, 38
Archaeological Institute of America (AIA), 36, 105, 106
archaeology: claims to the past nonexclusive, 2–3; incompatible with private collecting, 86; issue of using looted objects in, 4–5; as study of present, 1
archaeology, classical: development of, 50; history of collecting of, 47; post–World War II revival of, 51–52; works with objects without context, 43, 54
archaeology, maritime, 82–83. *See also* shipwreck sites, Australia
Arkansas, 127–129
Association of Art Museum Directors (AAMD), 33, 37
Athenian pottery: exported to Etruria, 28; origin of passion for, 26; prices of, 31. *See also* Euphronios; Sarpedon krater
Atlantis Antiquities, 38
Australian and Netherlands Committee Concerning Old Dutch Shipwrecks (ANCODS), 71, 78–79

159

authenticity: assumed by public when artifact is exhibited, 119; more important than provenience for biblical artifacts, 112–113, 116; necessary for spiritual engagement with relic, 115–116; provenience best guarantor of, 110–111

Bâb edh-Dhrâ', 5; archaeological excavation at, 16–18; estimated revenue to looters of, 22–23; looting at, 17, 18; pottery supposedly from sold by antiquities dealers, 21–22; use of Google Earth to estimate looting at, 18–19
Bachofen, Johann Jakob, 56
Batavia shipwreck, 73–74, 86
Beazley, John, 53
Belize, 13
Bible, 116, 117
Biblical Archaeology Society (BAS), 144
biblical artifacts: authenticity more important than provenience for, 112–113, 116; certificates of authenticity for, 112; commodity value of, 113–15; metonymic quality of, 112; political context of, 116–124; as relics, 118; religious or spiritual aura of, 112; spiritual engagement with, 113, 116
Boardman, John, 32
Boni, Giacomo, 50
Bourdieu, Pierre, 124
Boy-God, 59
Bronze Age, Aegean: differences between Minoan and Mycenean religious practices in, 67; evidence for human sacrifice in, 66–67; feasting in, 68; overly zealous reconstructions of, 61; problematic comparisons in, 61–62; shift in interpretation of from artifacts to ritual space, 61; in teaching texts, 62–65; suggestions for what should be included in humanities texts on, 66–68; use of questionable objects in writing about, 60, 61–62. *See also* Evans, Sir Arthur J.; Knossos, Crete
Bronze Age, Early (EBA): London market for pottery from, 20–21; price for pottery from, 20, 21. *See also* Bâb edh-Dhrâ'
Brooklyn Museum of Art, 55
Bulgaria, 93, 98, 99–100
Burke, Dolores L., 12, 14, 22, 23
Bürki, Fritz, 38
Butcher, Kevin, 101

Canadian Museums Association, 121
Carroll, Lewis, 1
Cenere, Armando, 26
Center for the Study of Democracy, 98
Cerveteri, Italy, 27, 28, 30, 34
Cicero, 45
classical archaeology. See archaeology, classical
Cleveland Museum of Art, 33
collecting/collectors, private: history of, 47; incompatible with archaeology, 86; professional restorers cater to, 128
collective memory, 116, 117
connoisseurship, shallow vs. informed, 3
context: in antiquities trade, 52–53; archaeological may be lost but other contexts replace it, 43, 44; of collection history for individual pieces, 47; creation of by archaeology connoisseur, 50–51; de Montebello on insignificance of archaeological context for understanding Greek vase painting, 33; Fascist ideological, 51; political, of biblical artifacts, 116–124; provenience as most reliable guarantor of authenticity, 110–111; sacred not lost, 44–45; "truth and beauty" as exalted, 54
Coptic sculpture, 55

Costa Rica, 10, 12, 13
Cunningham, Lawrence, 64–65
Cuno, James, 37–38, 40, 54
Cyprus, 102, 103

Davis, Hester A., 128
de Montebello, Philippe, 32–33
Discus Thrower, 45
Dunbar shipwreck, 76, 78
Dyson, Stephen L., 41–42

Elgin, Lord, 48–49
Elmali Hoard, 92
Etruscans, 26, 28, 29–30
Euphronios, 26, 30, 40; dates of, 29; find-spots for kraters attributed to, 27–28; as painter of Sarpedon krater, 31
Euxitheos, 31–32
Evans, Sir Arthur J.: argued authenticity of fake object with another fake, 59; core concepts of Minoan religion of, 56; fanciful reconstructions of Knossos of, 64–65; problematic methods of, 57, 60; use of fakes by, 58–59; use of misreconstructed pieces by, 57, 58; use of unprovenienced pieces by, 57. *See also* Knossos, Crete

fakes: of Coptic sculptures, 55–56; in Latin America, 132; of lithic artifacts, 131–132; Minoan, 58–59; prevalence of, 129; produced to match Evans' model of Minoan religion, 59. *See also* James Ossuary
Fayfa', Jordan, 23
Die Fundmünzen der römischen Zeit in Deutschland (FMRD), 96
Furtwangler, Adolph, 50

Gage, Nicholas, 26
Gandhara, 33
Getty Museum, J. Paul, 25, 26, 37, 39, 52

Gill, David, 101
Golan, Obed, 110, 114, 115, 122
Google Earth, 9. 14–15
Gorecki, Joachim, 95
Goulandris, Nicholas P. Foundation, 63
Greece, 39: nationalism and archaeological past in, 49. *See also* Athenian pottery; Euphronios

Hamilton, Sir William, 26
Heath, Dwight B., 9–10, 13
Hecht, Robert E., Jr., 26, 38
heritage law, denial of economic value in, 10–11. *See also* names of individual laws and conventions
Hermes of Praxiteles, 45
Historic Shipwrecks Act, 71, 72, 79: amnesty period for, 83–84; blanket protection of, 80, 89n4; custody transfer of relics and, 81, 84–86, 87–88; monetary rewards provision in, 81; protected zones and, 80
Historic Shipwrecks Inspector Training, 76, 89n2
Hollowell, Julie, 10, 12, 13
Homer, 30
Hoving, Thomas, 31

International Council of Museums (ICOM), 121–122, 123
Israel, 12; government licensed antiquities shops in, 112; lack of demand for Islamic artifacts in, 117–118; tourism in, 117. *See also* James Ossuary
Israel Antiquities Authority (IAA), 117–118, 122
Italy: attempts to get return of antiquities from European museums by, 34–35; display of returned antiquities in, 39–40; Greek pots from, 28; return of looted items to, 25, 38. *See also* Rome

James Ossuary: commercial potential of, 114–115; finder of charged with forgery and illicit trafficking in artifacts, 110; first public display of, 109–110, 114; first recognition of significance of, 114; issue of museum ethics in display of, 119–123; major concern about authenticity of but little about provenience of, 110, 113, 115
Jeffery, W., 87
Jehoash Tablet, 110
Jordan: low remuneration of diggers in, 12–14, 22–24; map of, 16; market for Early Bronze Age pottery from, 20–22; Roman-Byzantine cemeteries in, 14; study of site looting in, 15–19. *See also* Bâb edh-Dhrâ'

Kersel, Morag M., 112, 118
Knossos, Crete: evidence of human sacrifice at, 66; fanciful or incorrect reconstructions of, 64–65; Linear B tablets at, 67–68; problems with Evans' interpretation of, 56–59. *See also* Evans, Sir Arthur J.

Laocoon, 47
Lapatin, Kenneth, 59, 63
Lapp, Paul, 16–17
Latour, Bruno, 124
Lemaire, André, 109, 114
Levy, Leon, 27
looted antiquities: acquisition of encourages further looting, 38; in antiquity, 34; difference between remuneration of diggers and price on market, 11, 12–13; issue of cut off date for returning, 36–37, 39; knowledge lost from unpublished, 5; lose archaeological context but acquire others, 43, 44; professionals restrict publication of, 4. *See also* antiquities trade
looters: knowledge of archaeology of, 20; suggested term "subsistence diggers" for, 10; wages of, 22. *See also* subsistence diggers/digging
looting: as economic stimulus for local economy, 13, 14; of Greco-Roman sites in Renaissance, 46–47; of small benefit to general public in Jordan, 23–24. *See also* subsistence diggers/digging
Lydian hoard, 41, 92

Martin, Chris, 20–21
Mask of Agamemnon, 63, 65
Matthews, Roy, 64
McCane, Byron, 119
McGimsey, Charles R., 128
Medici, Giacomo, 27, 38, 40
Metropolitan Museum of Art, 25, 53; purchase of Sarpedon krater by, 26, 53; return of items to Italy by, 25, 39, 40
Minerva, 101–2
Minneapolis Institute of Arts, 25
Minoans. *See* Bronze Age, Aegean; Evans, Sir Arthur J.; Knossos, Crete
Mommsen, Theodor, 94–95
Morgantina silver hoard, 37, 41
Museum Act, Western Australia, 78, 79
Museum of Fine Arts, Boston, 25, 39
museums: claim of "scrupulous acquisition rules" of questioned, 32–33; as final resting place for looted antiquities, 37–38; as gatekeepers, 119; predominance of unprovenienced antiquities in, 33, 34; willingness of to turn a blind eye to provenience, 124. *See also* Royal Ontario Museum; names of individual museums
Mussolini, Benito, 51
Mycenaeans, 59–60

Nemea, Greece, 95
Nero, 45–46
New South Wales, 76–77
Nilsson, Martin, 59–60

Nimrud Ivories, 34
numismatics, two streams of study in, 94–95. *See also* ancient coins

Oltos, 32
Olympia, Greece, 45–46

Palaikastro, Crete, 66
past: exclusive vs. nonexclusive access to, 2; studied in the present, 1
Pausanias, 45
Persson, Axel W., 60
Petsophas, Crete, 66
Picón, Carlos, 41
Platt, DeWitt, 64
Pliny the Elder, 47
Politis, Konstantinos D., 21, 22, 23
Pollock, Susan, 113
Princeton University Art Museum, 25, 27, 39
provenience: overshadowed by issues of authenticity in the Holy Land, 110, 111, 113, 115; problems of theories based upon objects without, 57; rarely of interest to purchasers of biblical artifacts, 112–113, 116; used by dealers to increase historical interest in antiquities, 21–22
Pylos, Crete, 68

Queen of Nations shipwreck, 76

Reich, John, 64–65
Renaissance, identification with classical antiquity in, 46
Rollston, Christopher, 113
Roman Forum, 50
Romans: copies of Greek originals made for, 45, 46; looting of art by, 44
Rome: Italian government attempt to link to glories of ancient, 49–50; recycling of Greco-Roman statuary fragments in Christian, 46
Rose, Jerome C., 12, 14, 22, 23

Royal-Athena Galleries, 25, 39
Royal Ontario Museum (ROM): economic benefit of ossuary exhibit to, 123–124; exhibit of James Ossuary by, 109–110, 114, 121; failed gatekeeper duty of, 119; failed to establish ownership of James Ossuary, 122–123; objectives of, 120; pressure on to exhibit James Ossuary, 123

St. Lawrence Island, 12, 13, 23
Sarpedon krater, 6, 53; dating of, 29; as high art?, 31–32; history of acquisition of, 26–27; inscription on, 29; interpretation of iconography of, 29–30; return to Italy of, 25, 39, 40
Sarraifan, Dikran A., 26–27
Saslow, Arnold R., 101–102
Sayles, Wayne, 102
Sayre, Henry, 62, 63
Shanks, Hershel, 114–115, 119, 123
Shelmerdine, Cynthia, 61–62
shipwreck sites, Australia: archaeological importance of, 71; blanket protection concept for, 80, 89n4; illegal interference still occurs on, 87; legislation concerning custody transfer of relics from, 81, 84–86; problem of existing private collections from, 72, 76–77; protected zones around, 80; protective legislation for causes resentment with some in diving community, 86. *See also* names of individual shipwrecks
Snake Goddess, 57–58, 59, 63, 64, 65
Solomon, First Temple of, ivory pomegranate from, 110, 112, 114
Staley, David P., 10
State Maritime Archaeology Act, 79
subsistence diggers/digging, 10; potential for reducing in Jordan, 24; remuneration of, 11, 12–14
Symes, Robin, 39

Thorsell, William, 122
tradition, 116
Trial (*Tryall*) shipwreck, 74, 75
Tsountas, Christos, 63
Turkey, 12, 39, 52, 92, 101

UNESCO Convention on the Means of Prohibiting and Preventing the Illicit Import, Export and Transfer of Ownership of Cultural Property, 36, 37, 122–123
UNESCO Convention on the Protection of the Underwater Cultural Heritage, 85

Vaughn, Andrew G., 113

Vergulde Draeck shipwreck, 73
Victoria, Australia, 77, 79
Virú Valley, Peru, 20
von Kaenel, Hans-Markus, 94

Welsh, David, 103–104
Western Australian Museum, 74, 75
Williams, Dyfri, 29
William Salthouse shipwreck, 77, 79, 80
Winckelmann, Johannes, 48
White, Shelby, 25, 27, 36, 39
Whittaker, John C., 131

Zerubavel, Yael, 117
Zuytdorp shipwreck, 75–76, 77, 80